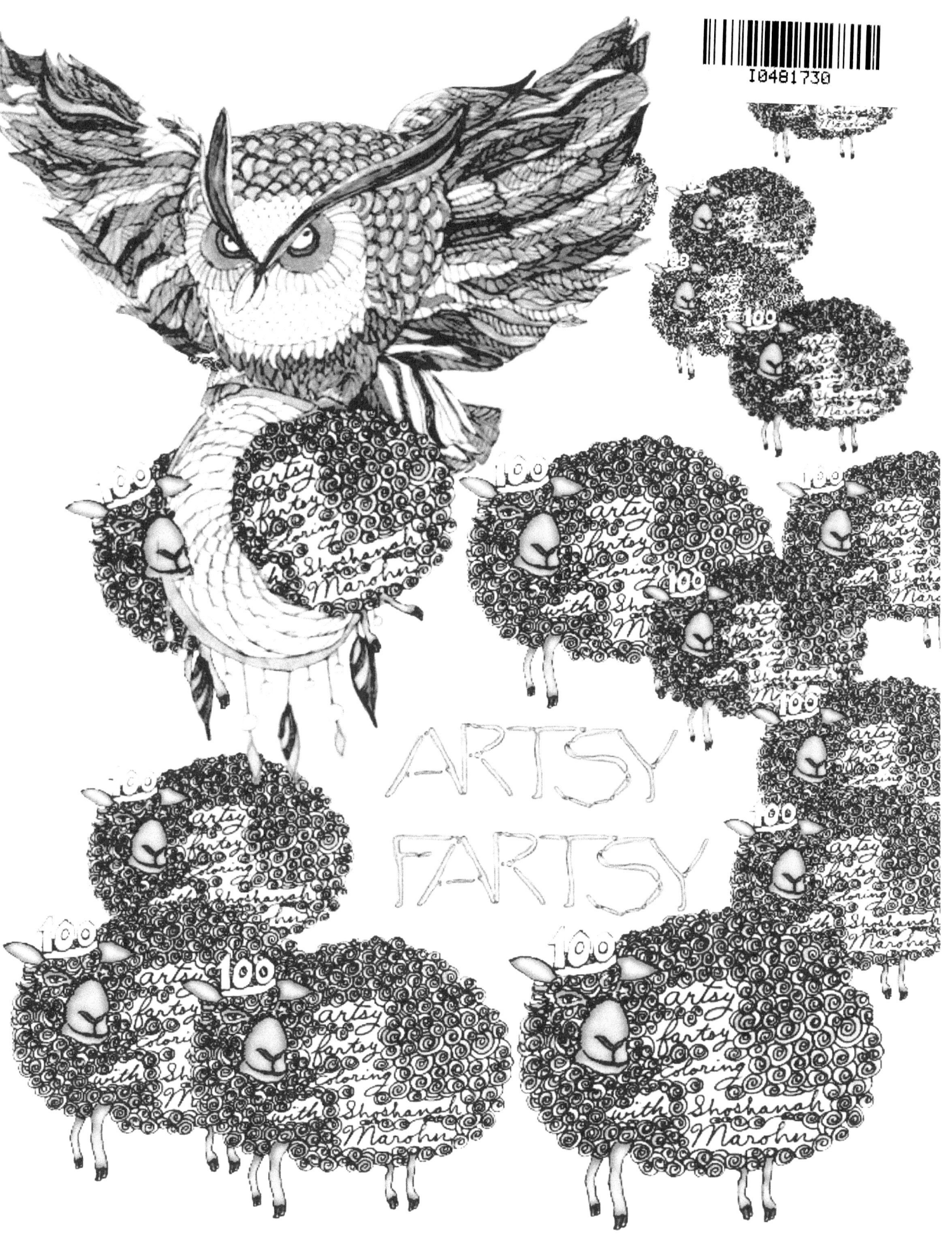

**ISBN-13:
978-1984952042**

**ISBN-10:
1984952048**

Cover art was a collaboration between Shoshanah Marohn, Gina Wenzel-Garza, and Nancy Haarbrink-van Der Werf.
Line drawing and collage by Shoshanah Marohn, owl coloring by Gina Wenzel-Garza, and sheep coloring by Nancy Haarbrink-van Der Werf.

Thank you to all of the members of the Facebook group, **Artsy Fartsy Coloring AND Colouring,** for making this possible. All 31 of the images in this book were originally drawn by me, Shoshanah Marohn, for members of that group to color. Many of them were drawn for the winners of "The Great Artsy Fartsy Facebook Takeover," which is a game we play within the group. Winners of the game get to request a free drawing, which is then drawn by me and shared with the entire group. Members have come up with some amazing ideas for me to draw, like the bush baby gangsters or the boxing kangaroo poster. The pictures in this group are diverse, because every one of the contest winners has a different idea of what she would like me to draw. I have loads of fun with this. I draw things I would never even have conceived of. I dare say the group members are having fun, too.

Those drawings started piling up, and one day I realized, *Hey! I've got enough drawings here for a whole coloring book!* This is that book.

These drawings were all free at one time to members of the Artsy Fartsy Coloring AND Coloring group. If you want to get these for free in the future, just join the group. It's at https://www.facebook.com/groups/artsyfartsycoloringANDcolouring/

We'd love to see how you colored these! Everyone is kind and supportive in the group. If they aren't, I kick them out. Join us! We're totally not a cult.

-Shoshanah Marohn

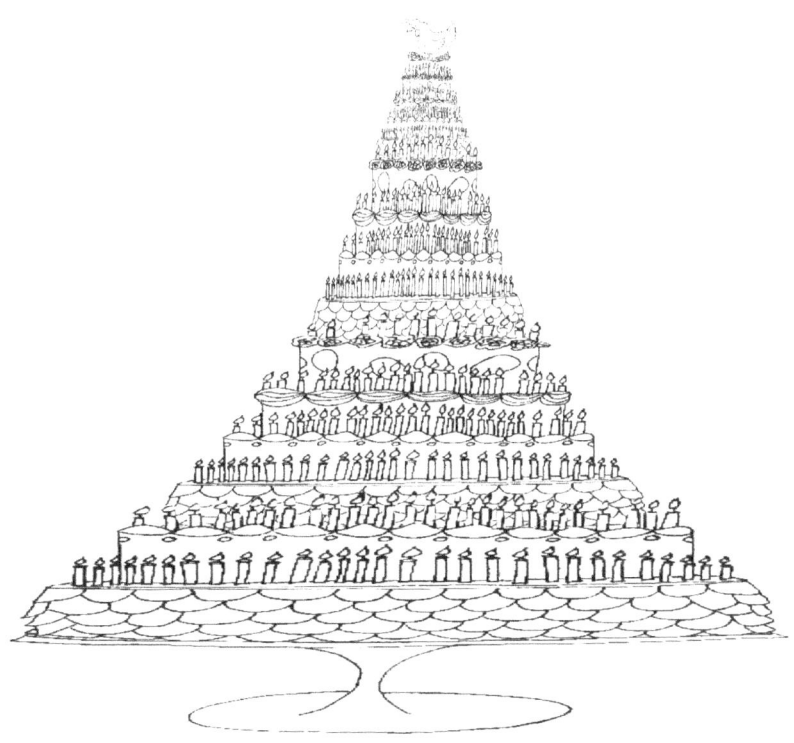

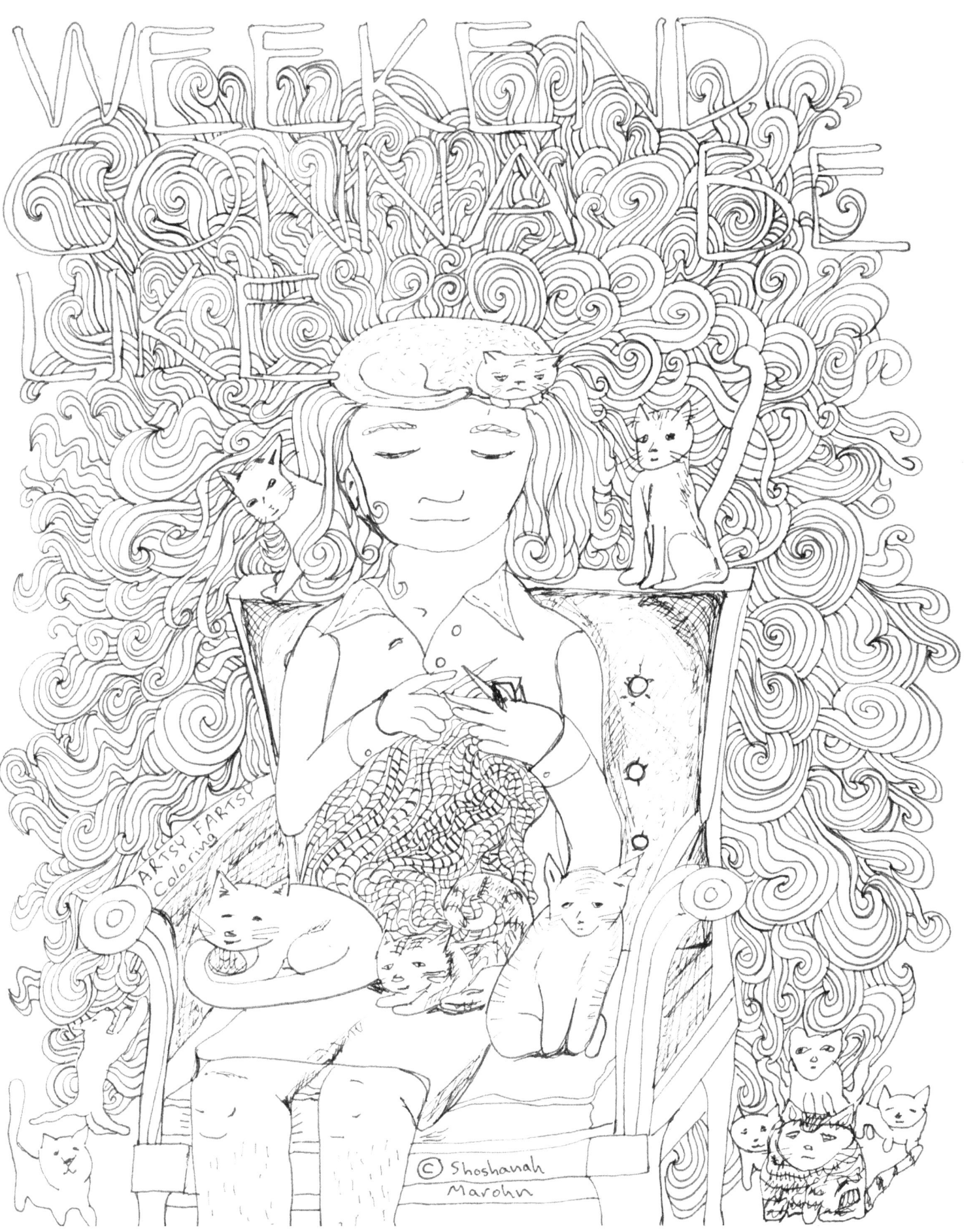

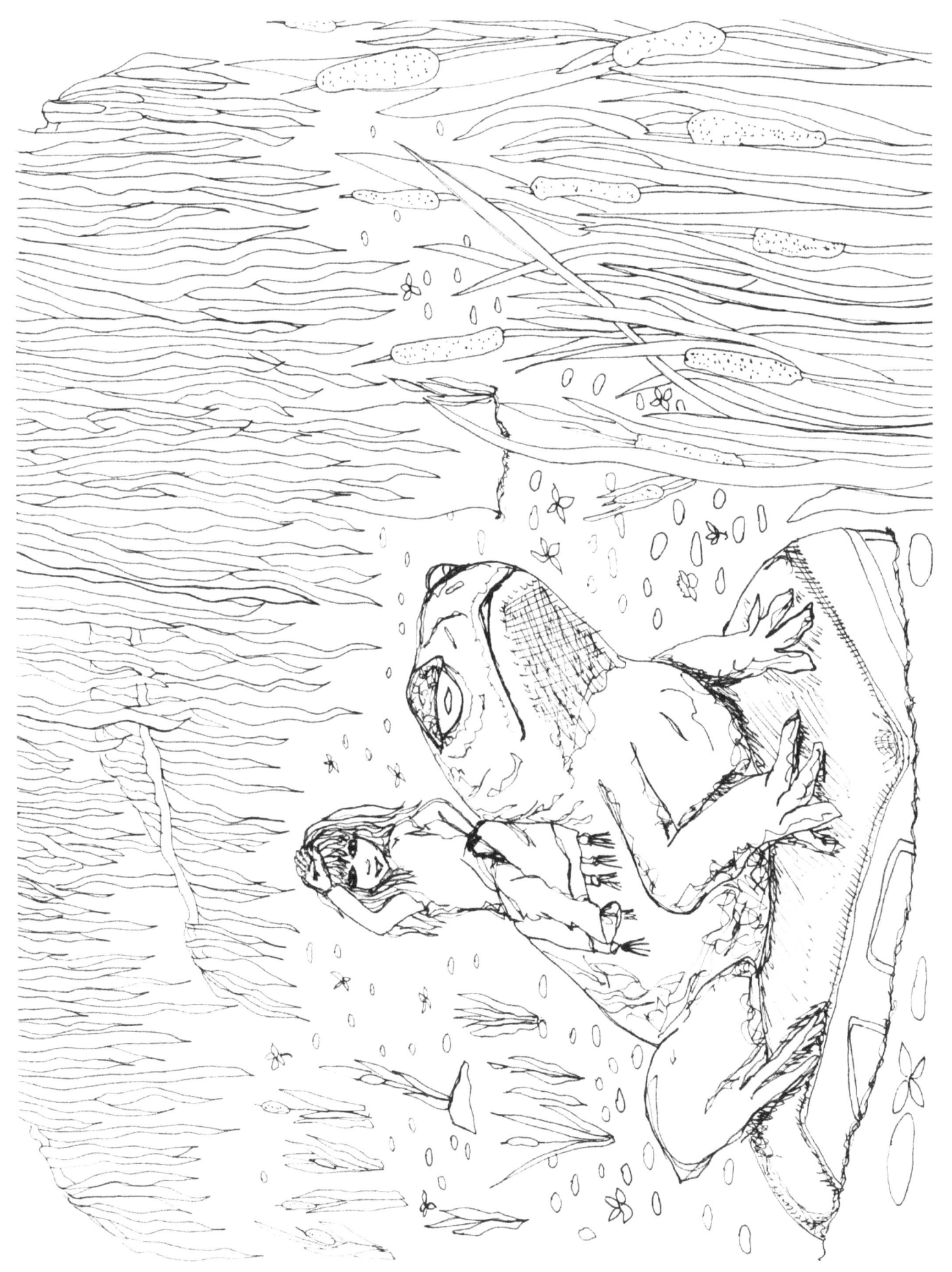

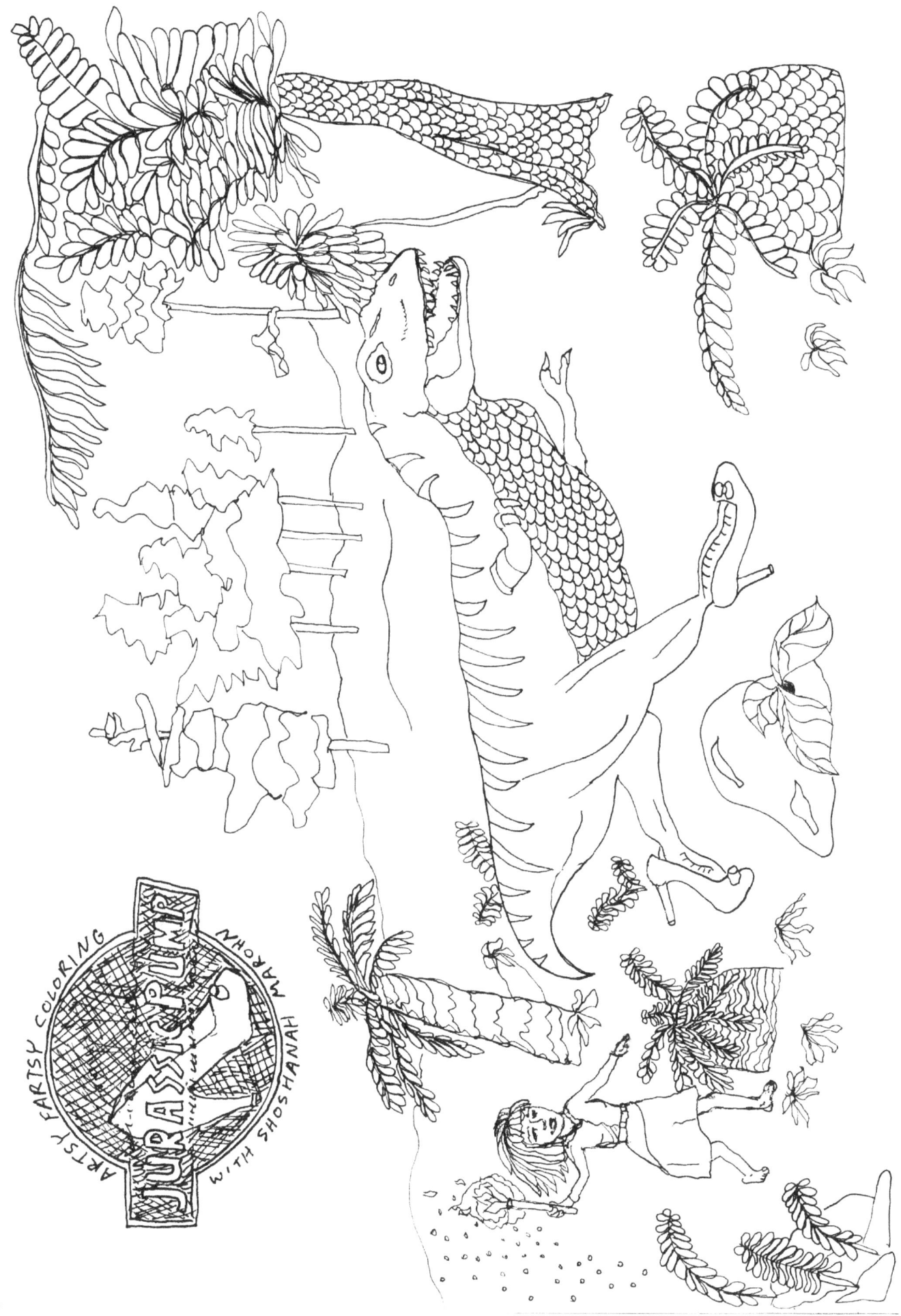

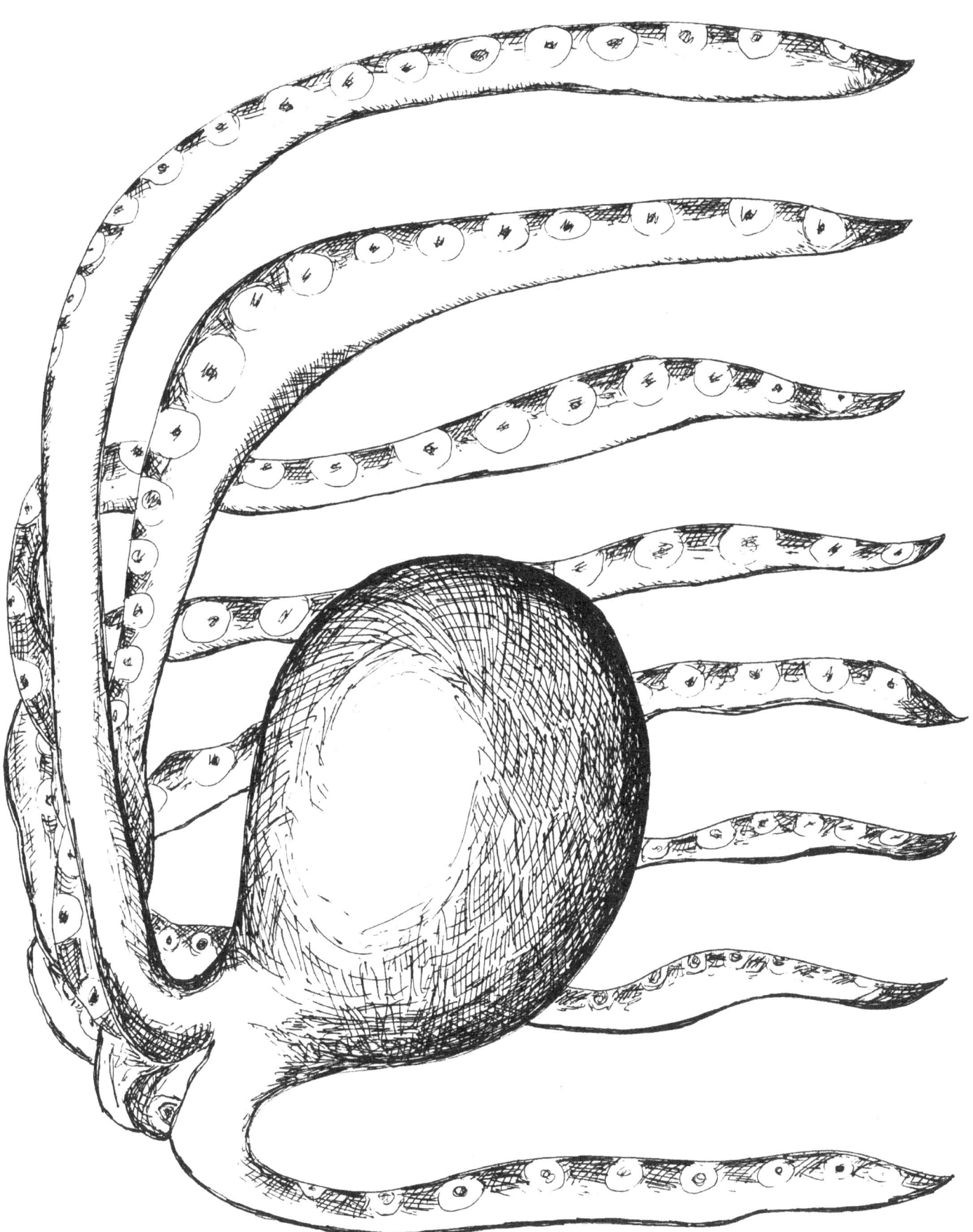

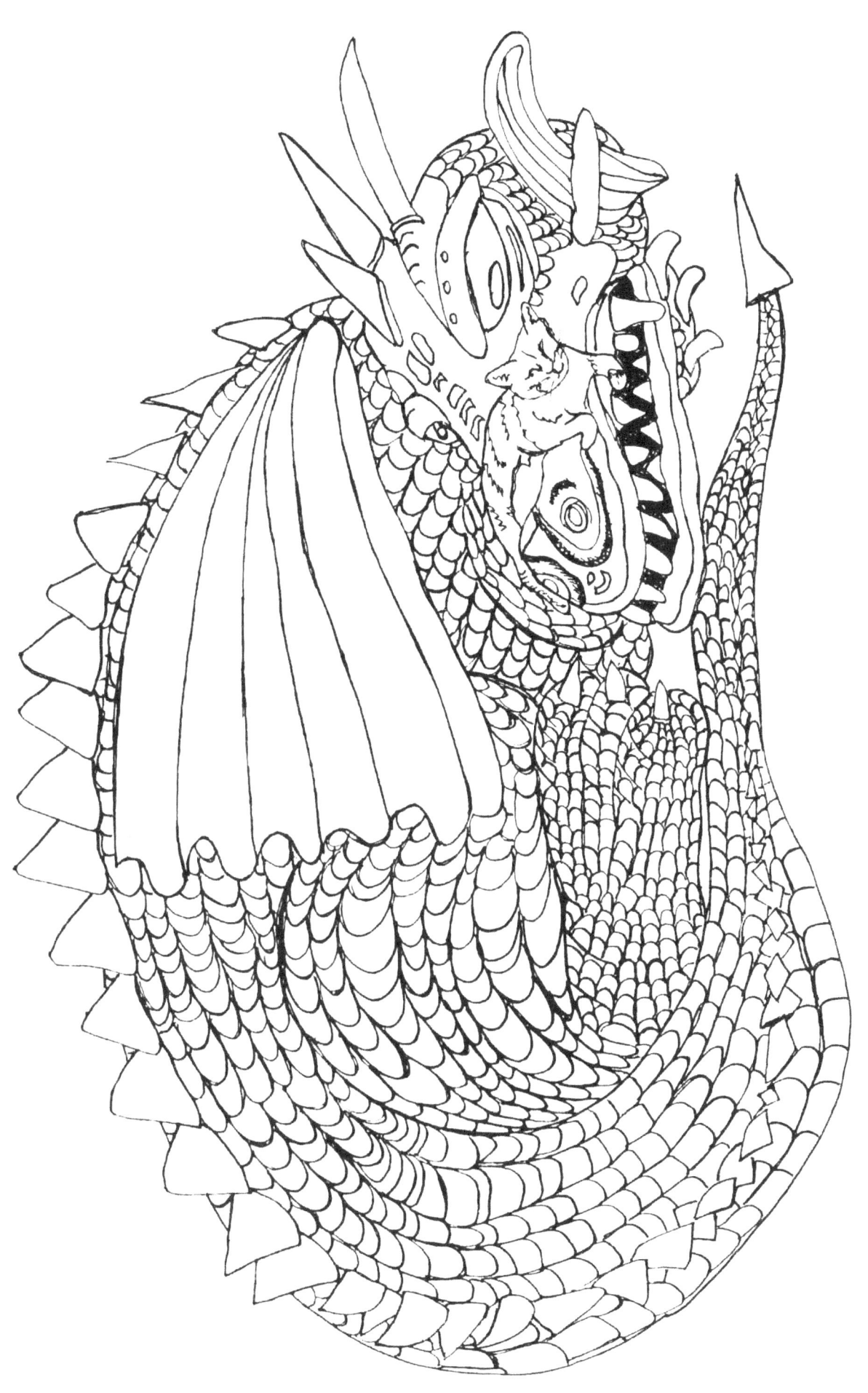

CHILLIN' LIKE A SLOTH ON A SUNDAY

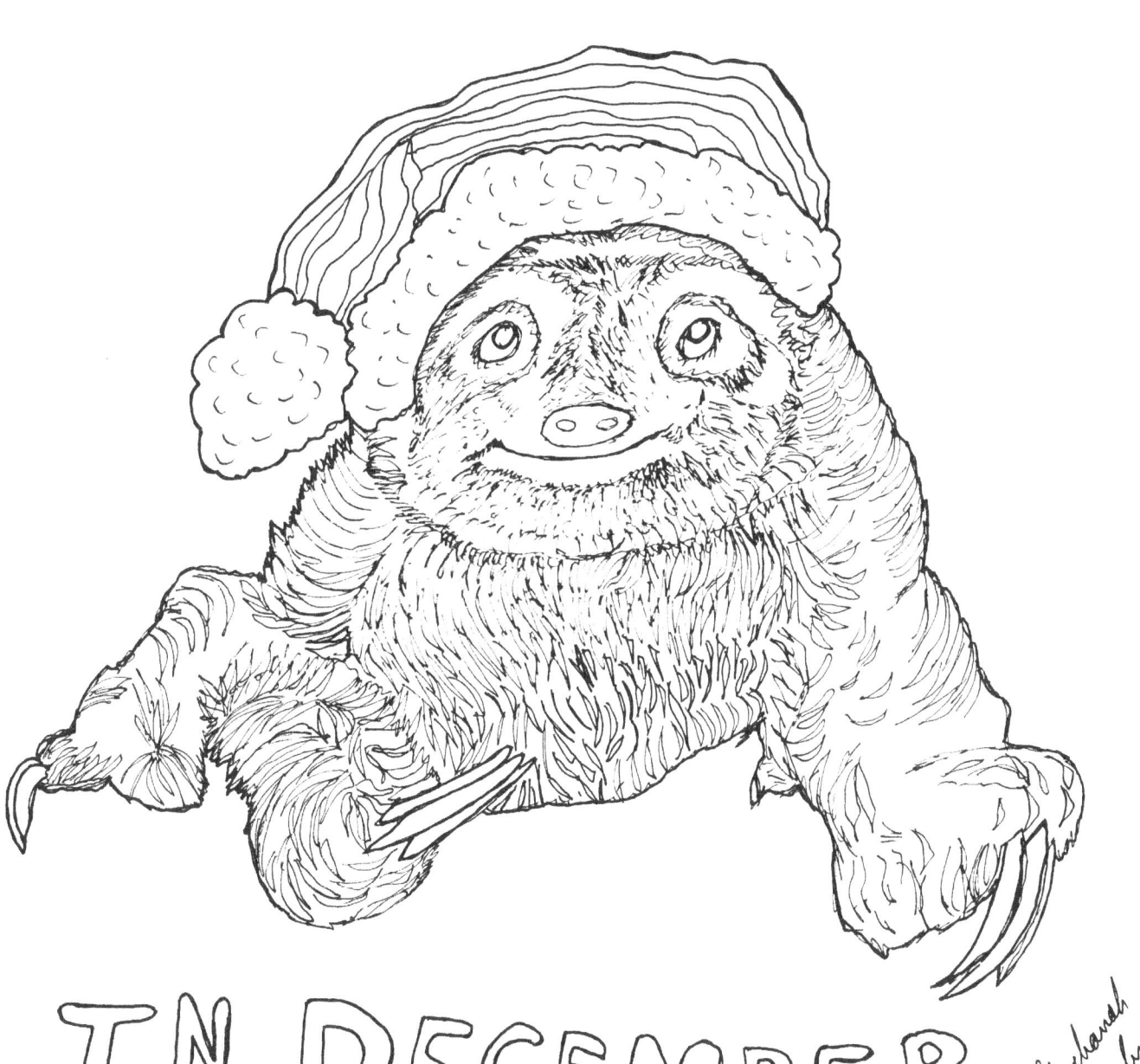

IN DECEMBER

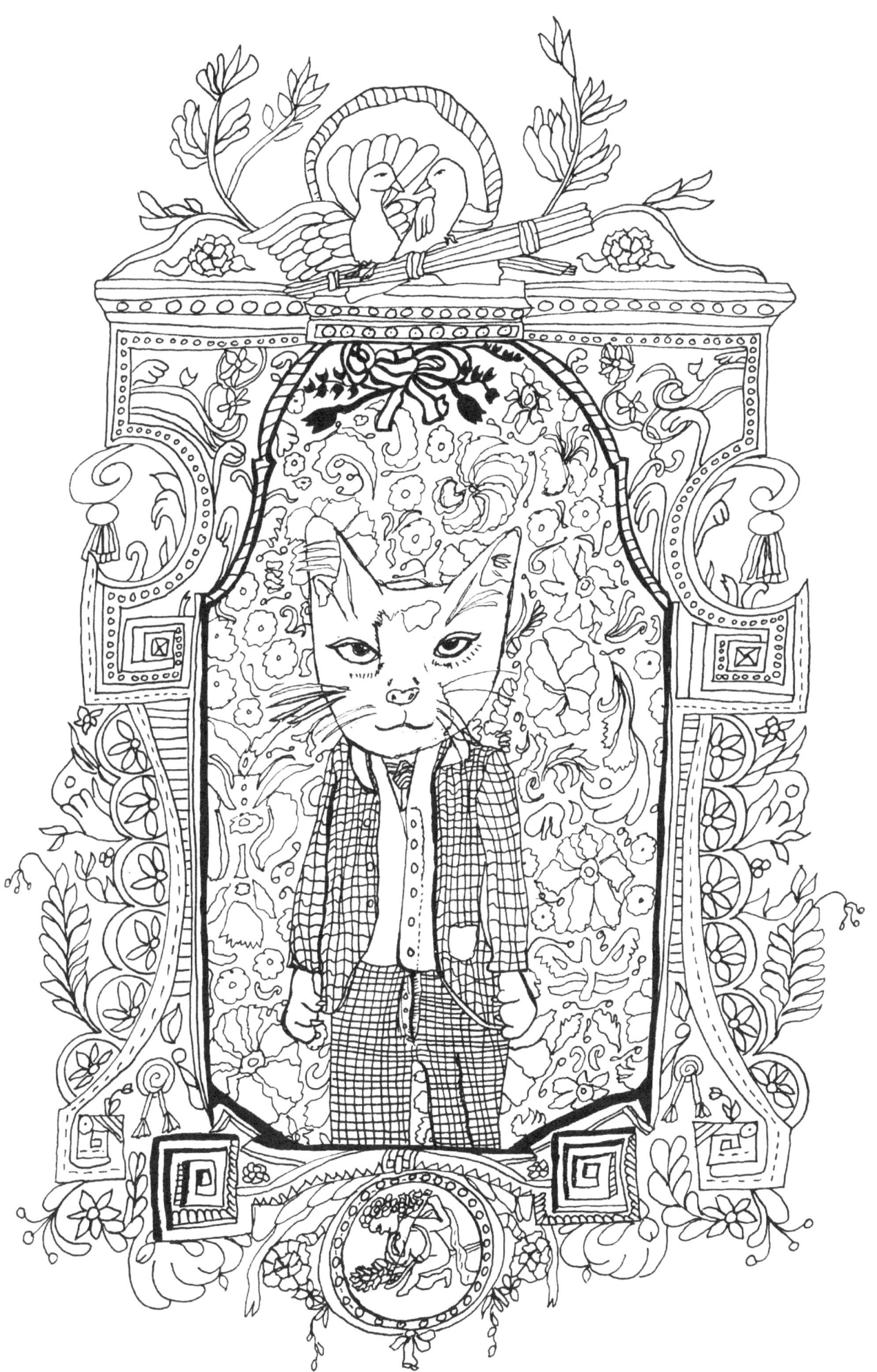

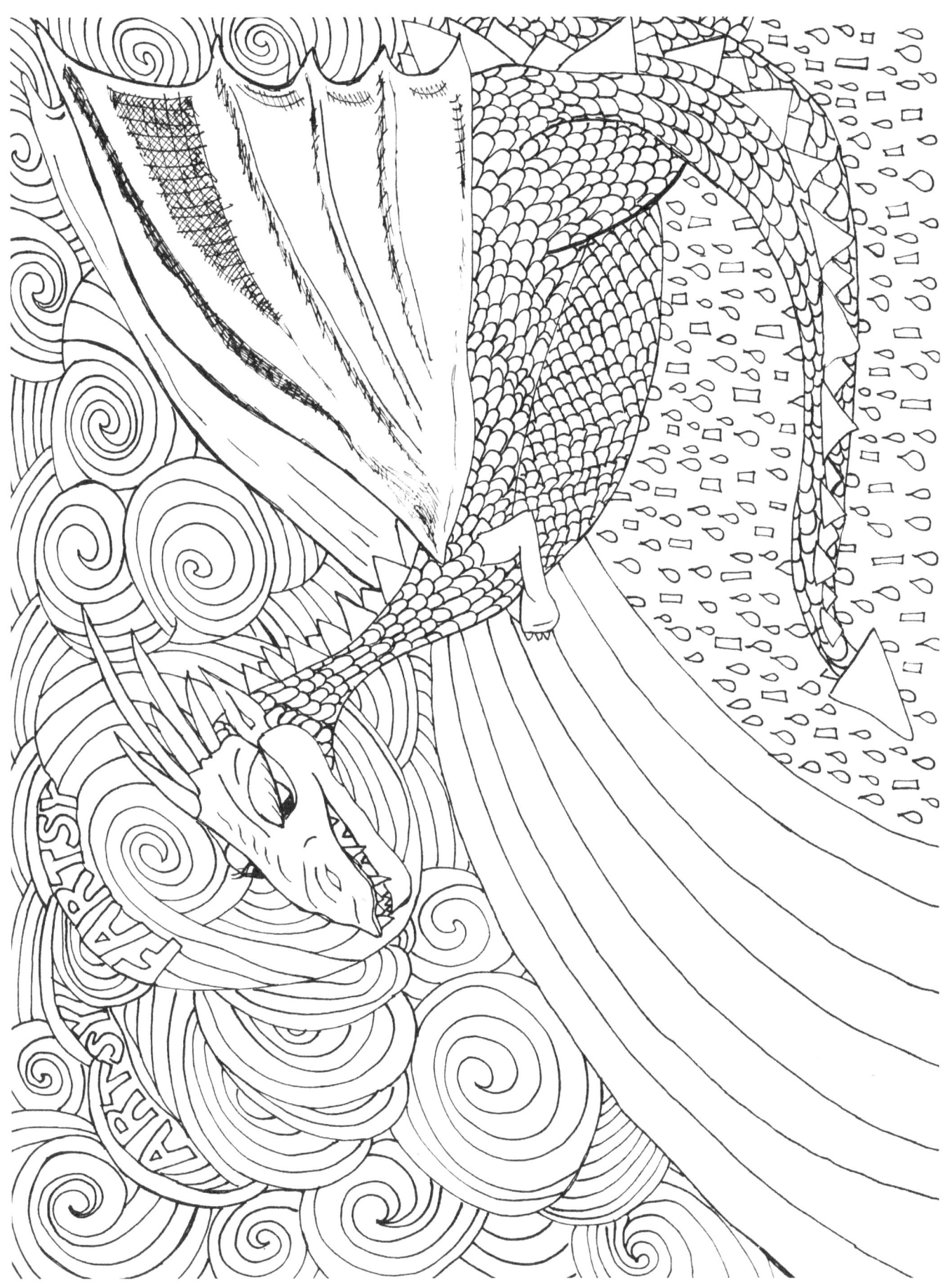

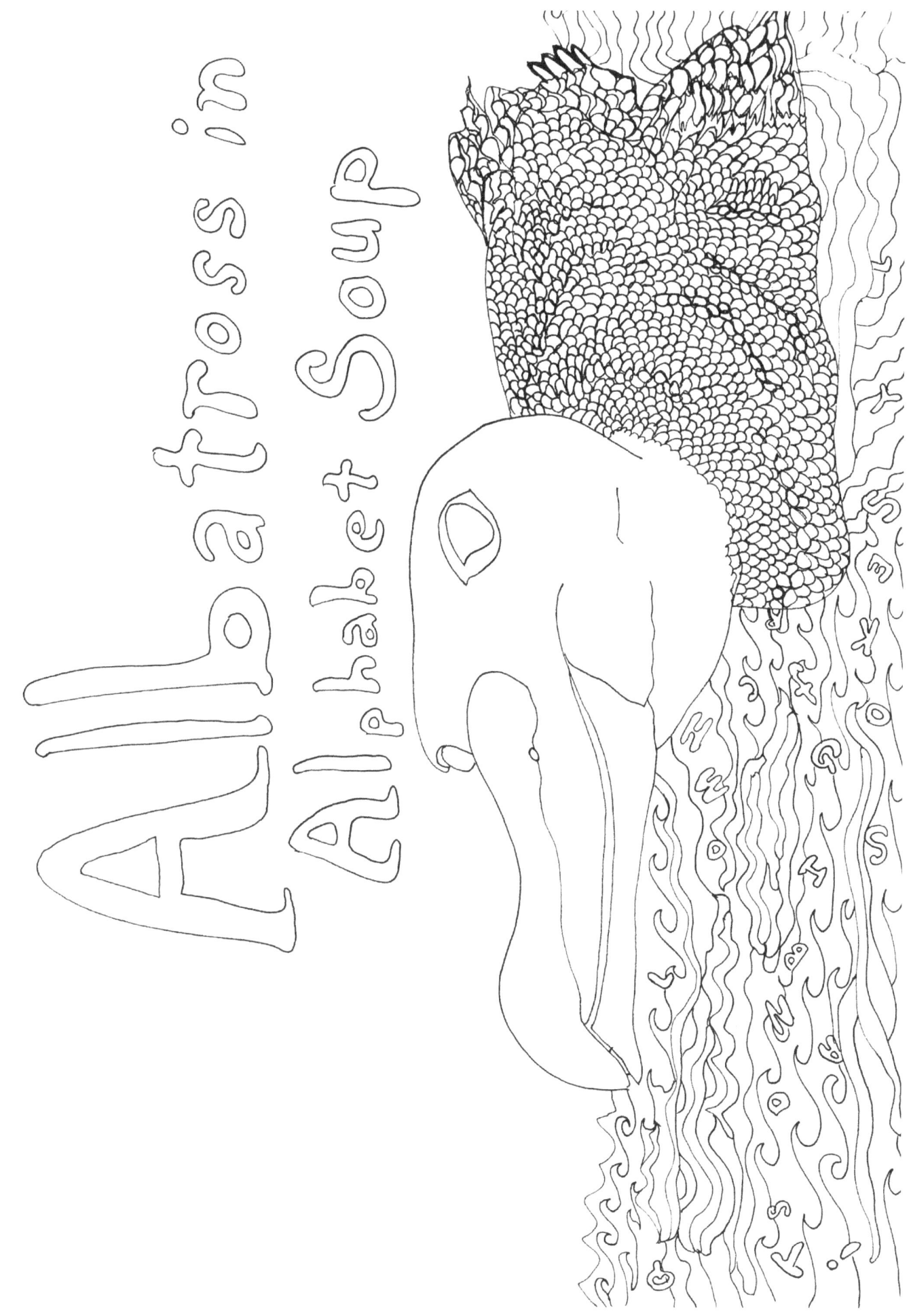

All batross in
Alphabet Soup

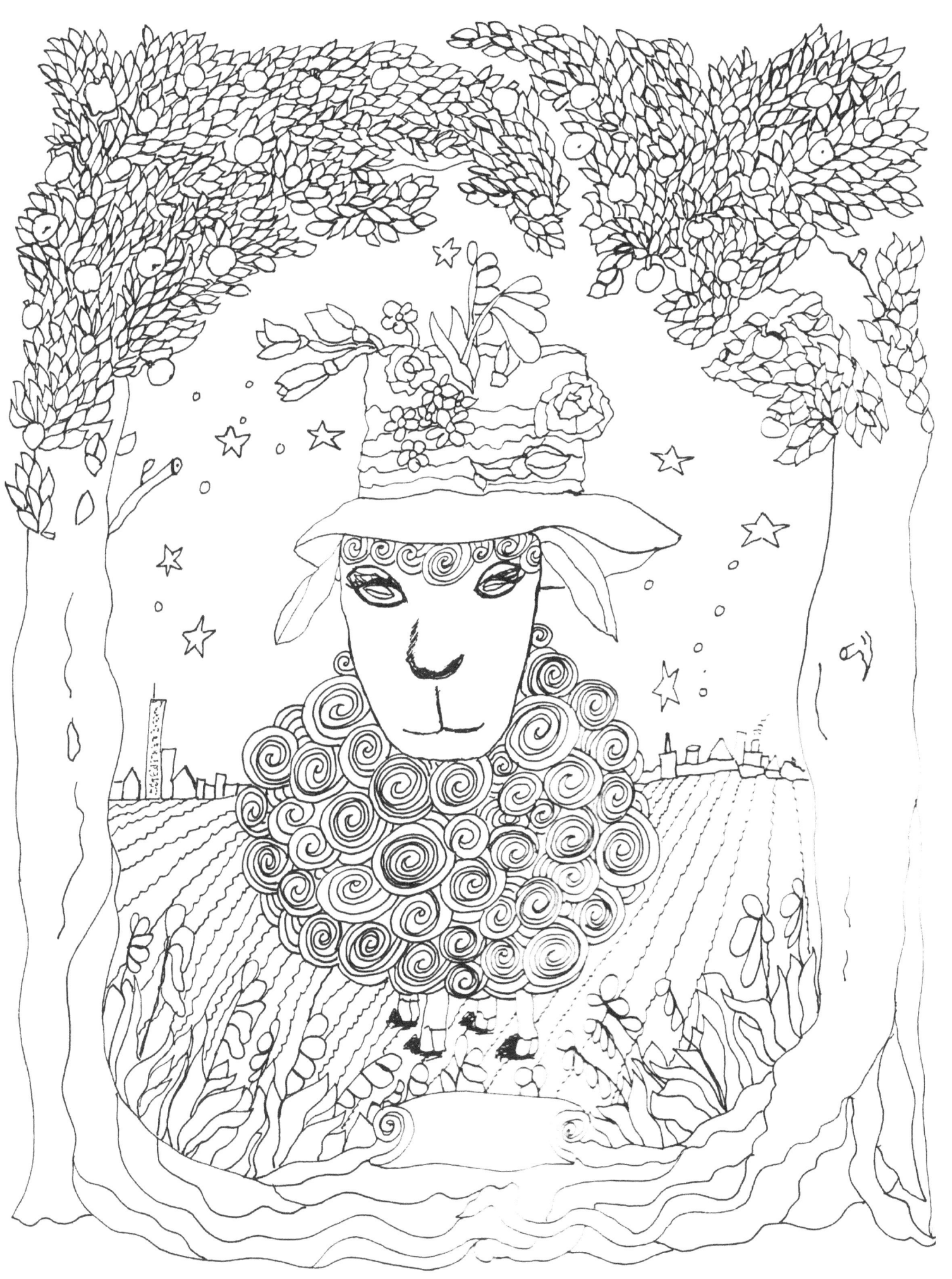

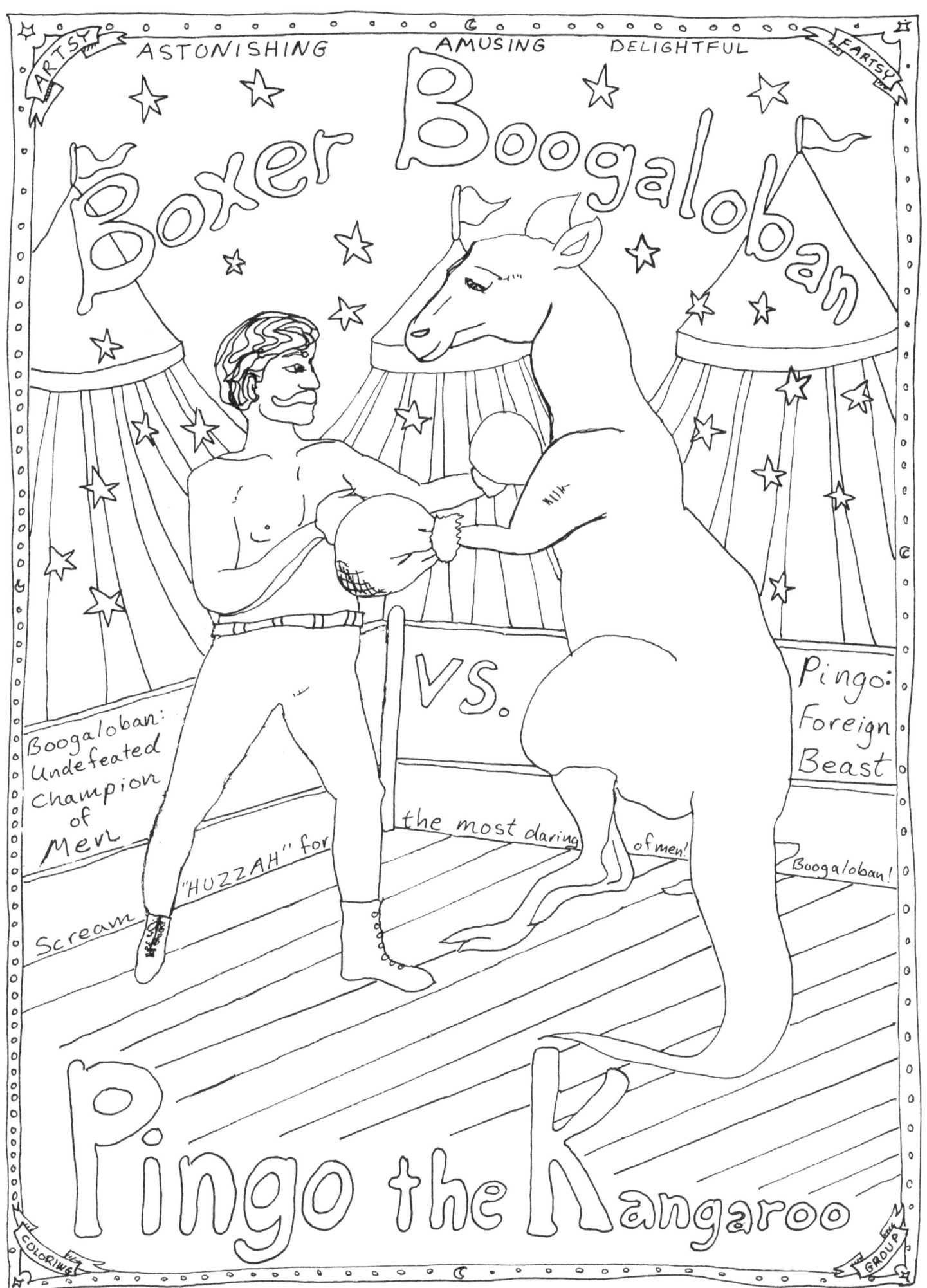

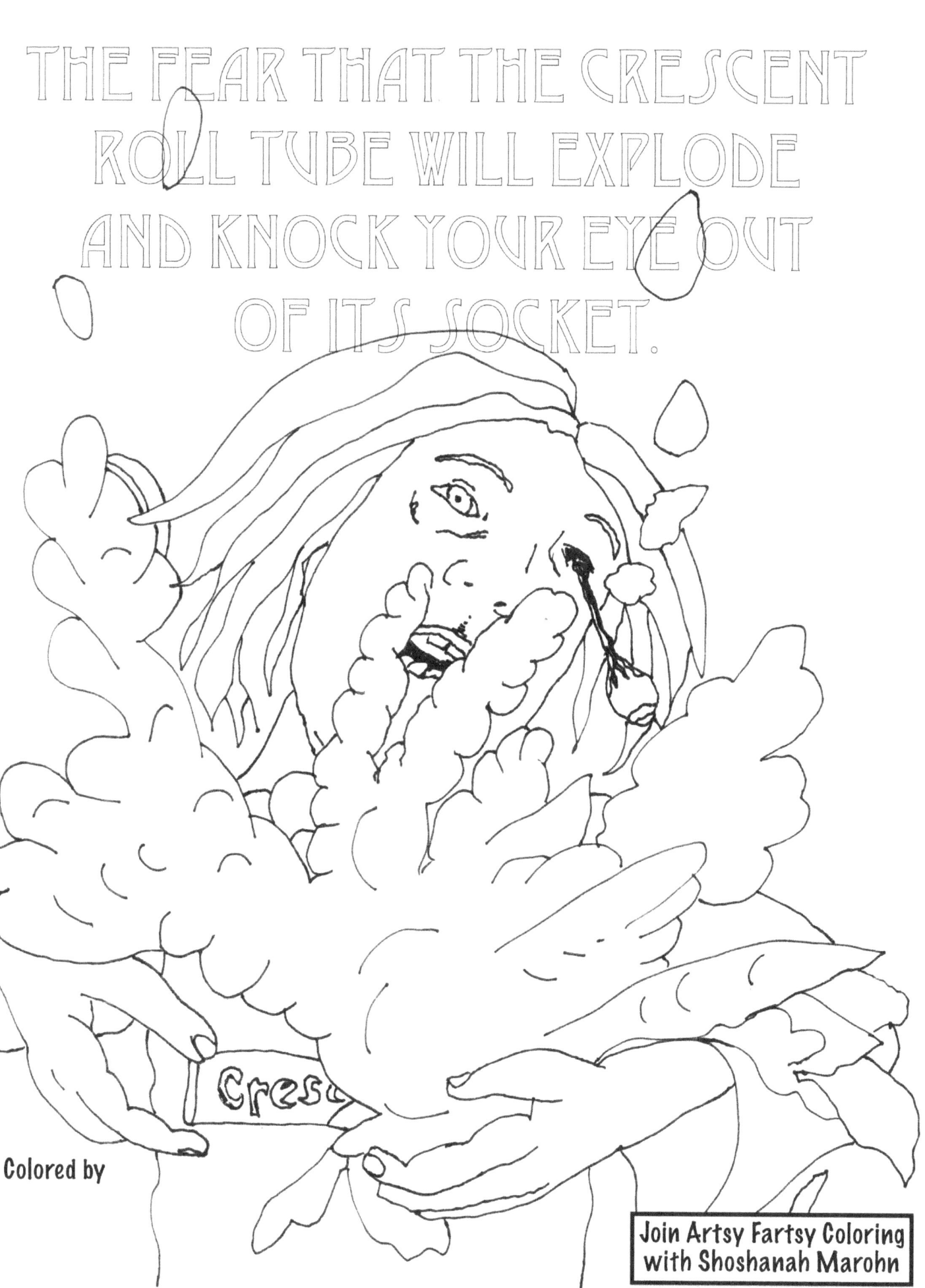

THE FEAR THAT THE CRESCENT ROLL TUBE WILL EXPLODE AND KNOCK YOUR EYE OUT OF ITS SOCKET.

Cresc

Colored by

Join Artsy Fartsy Coloring
with Shoshanah Marohn

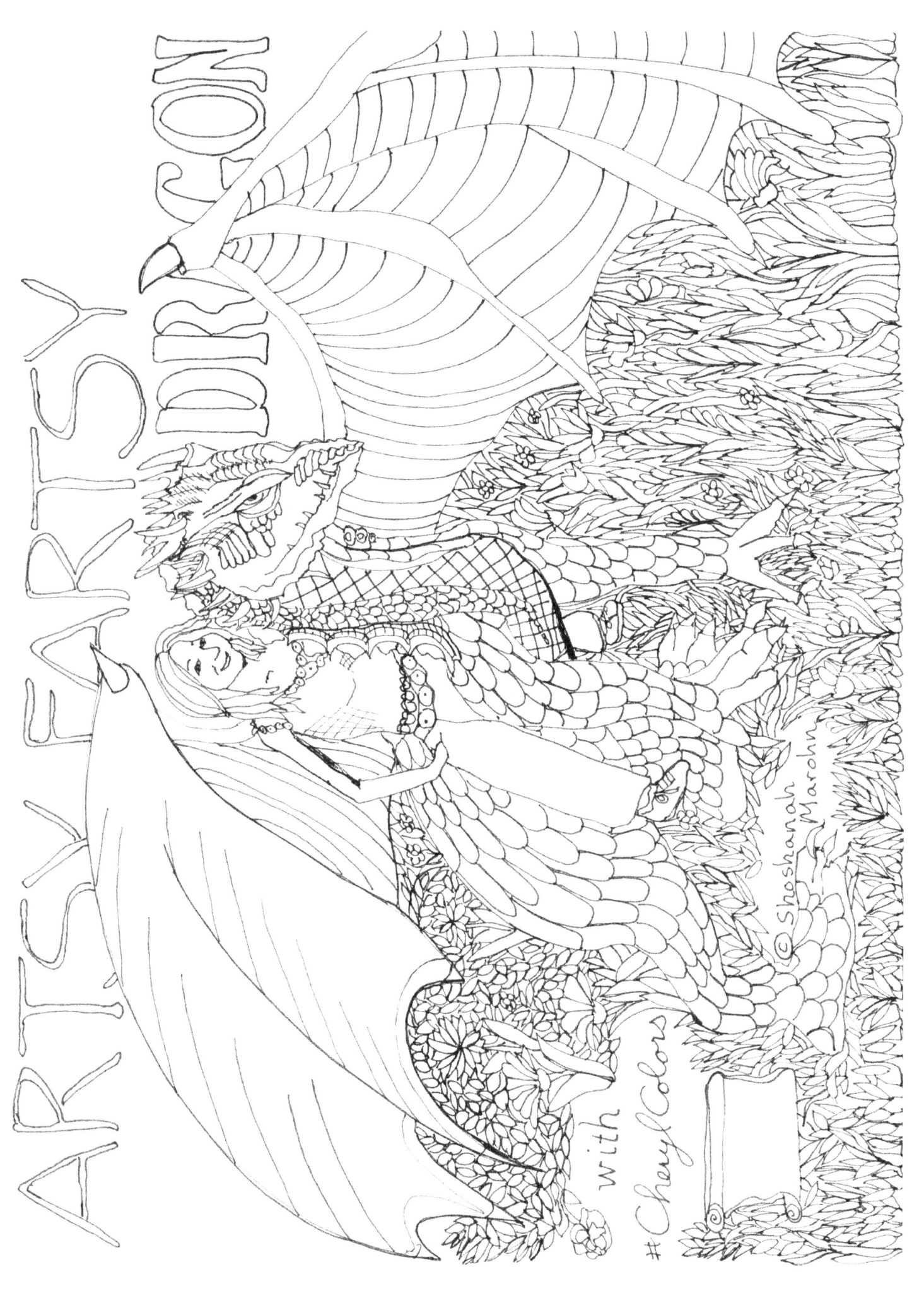

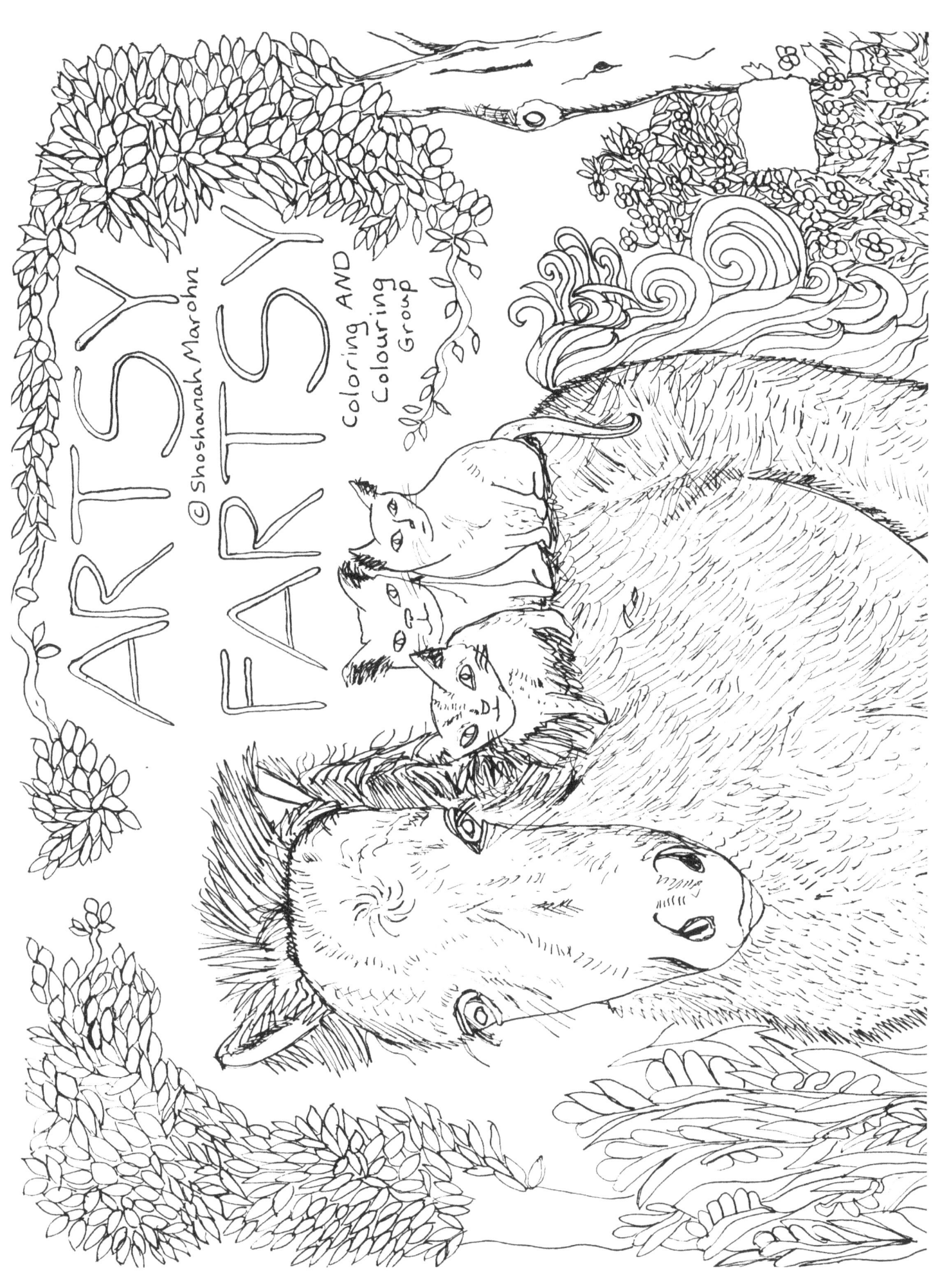

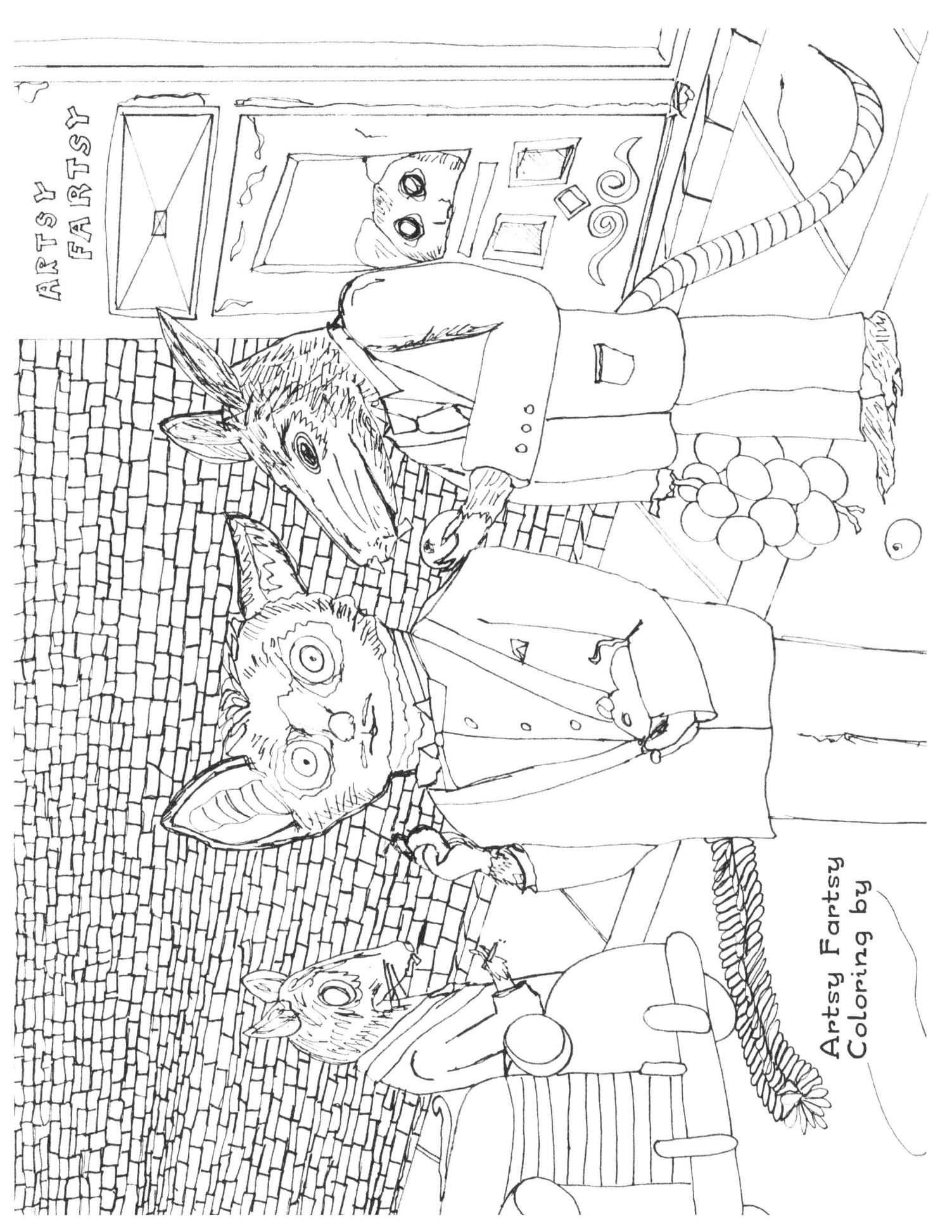

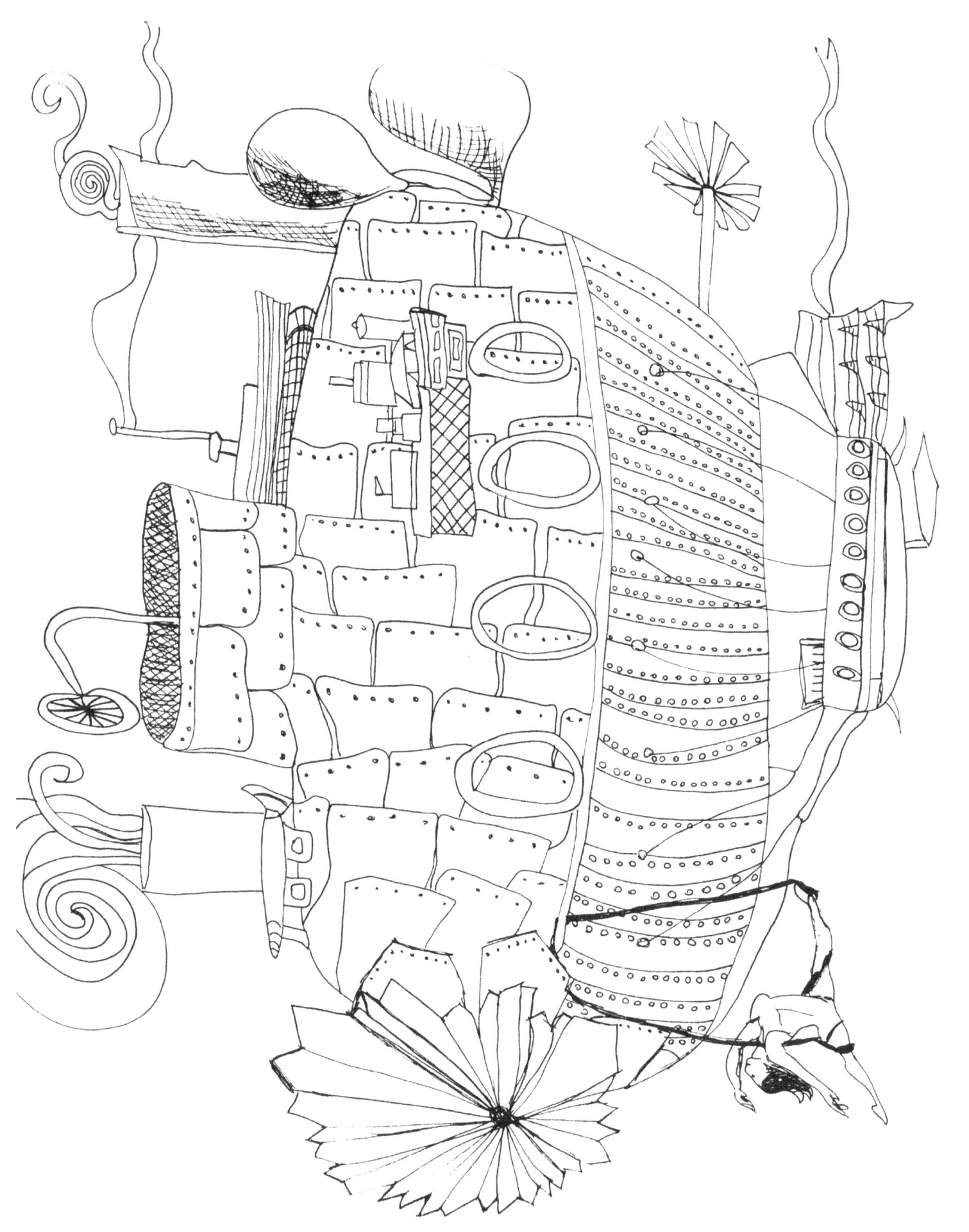

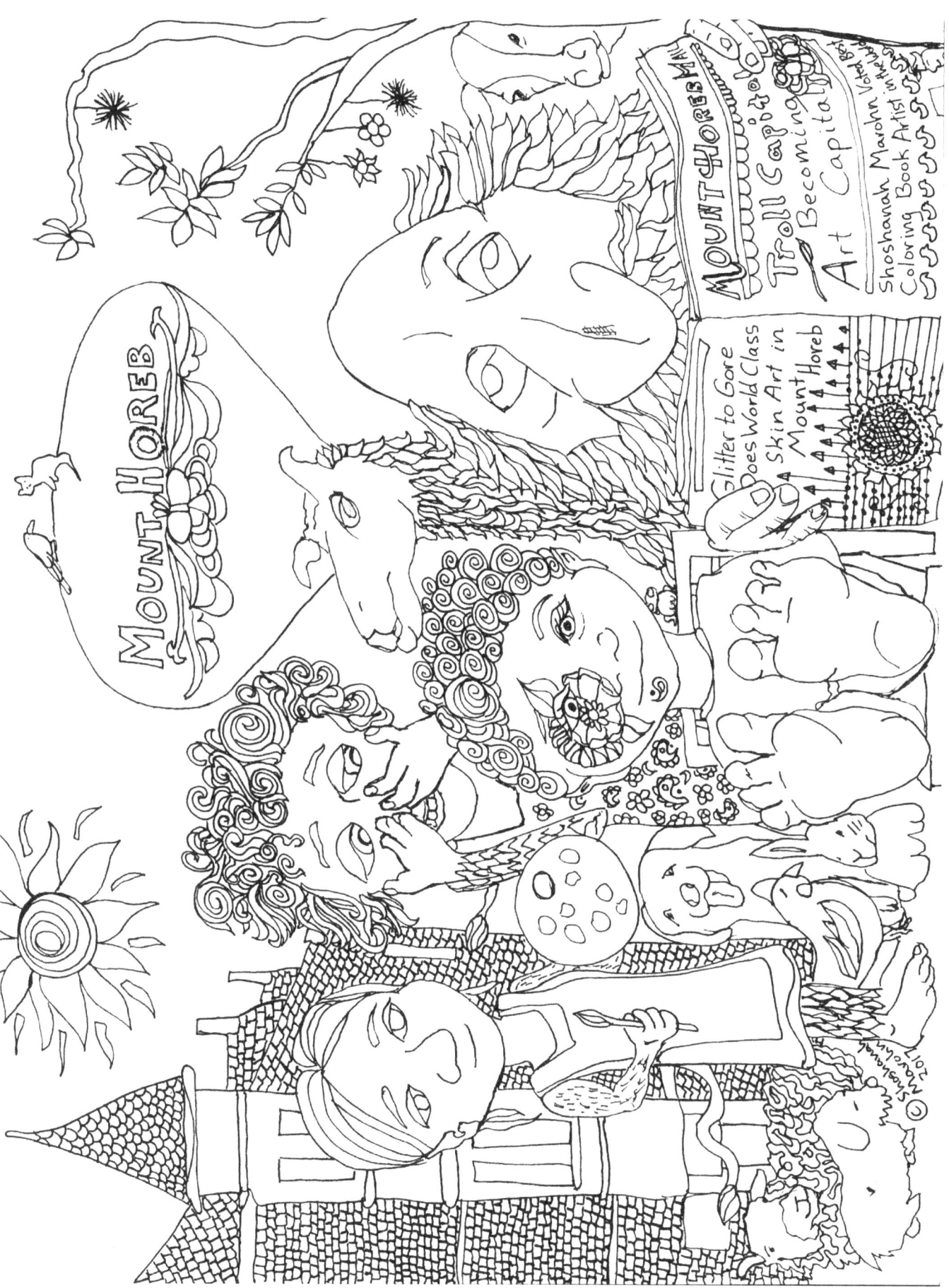

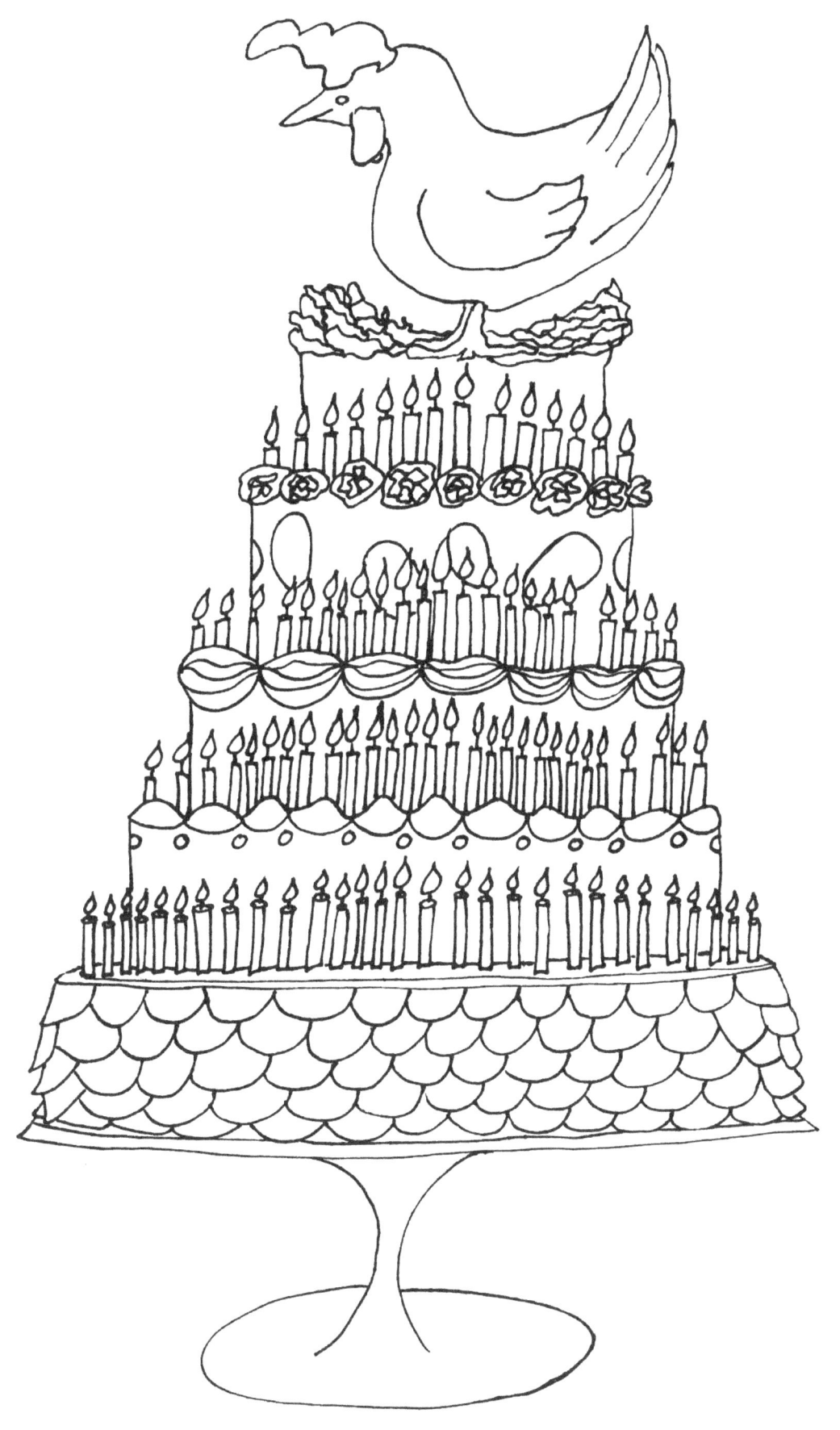

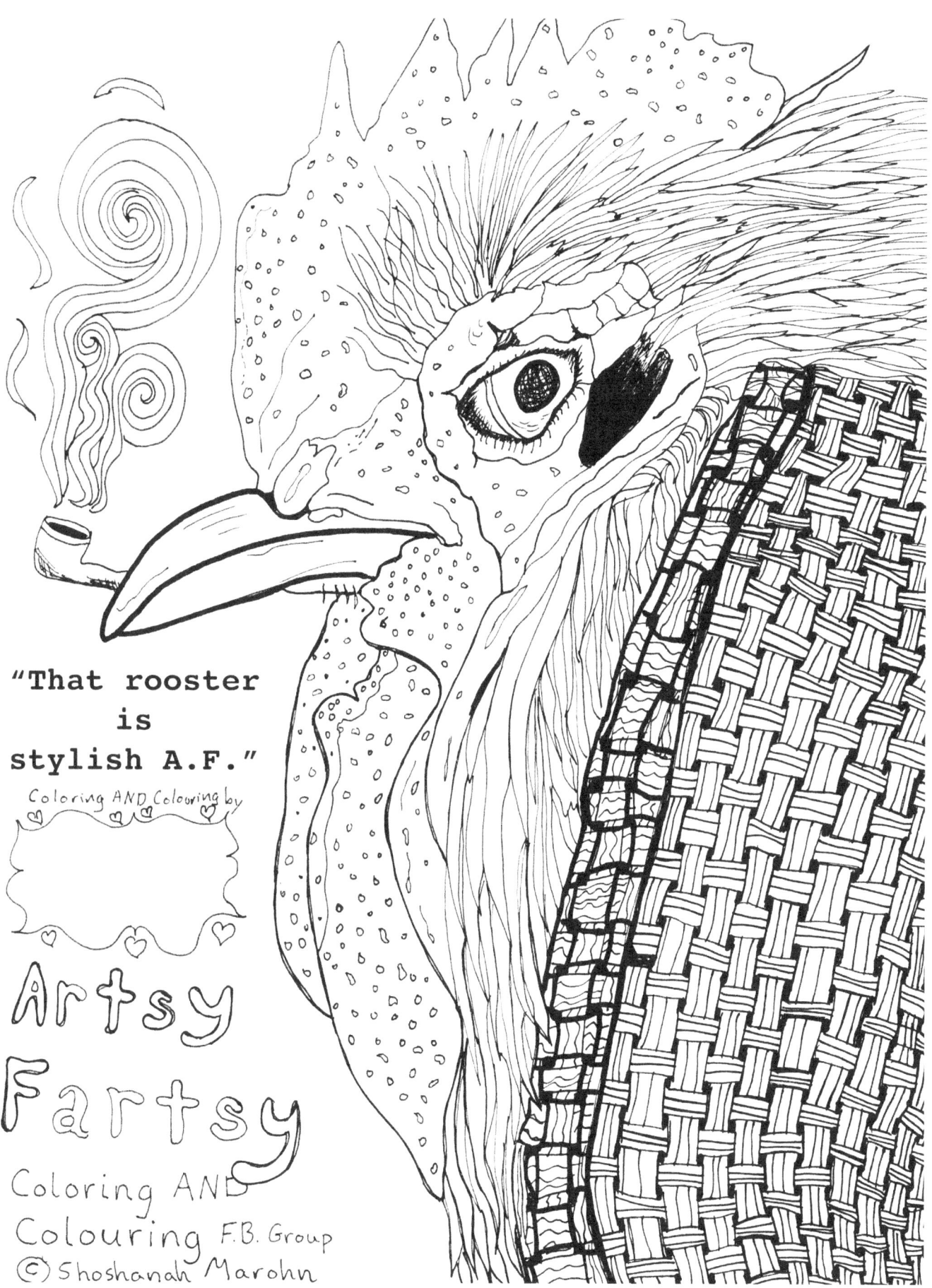

"That rooster is stylish A.F."

Coloring AND Colouring by

Artsy Fartsy

Coloring AND Colouring F.B. Group
© Shoshanah Marohn

Artsy Fartsy Sheep in a Sweater

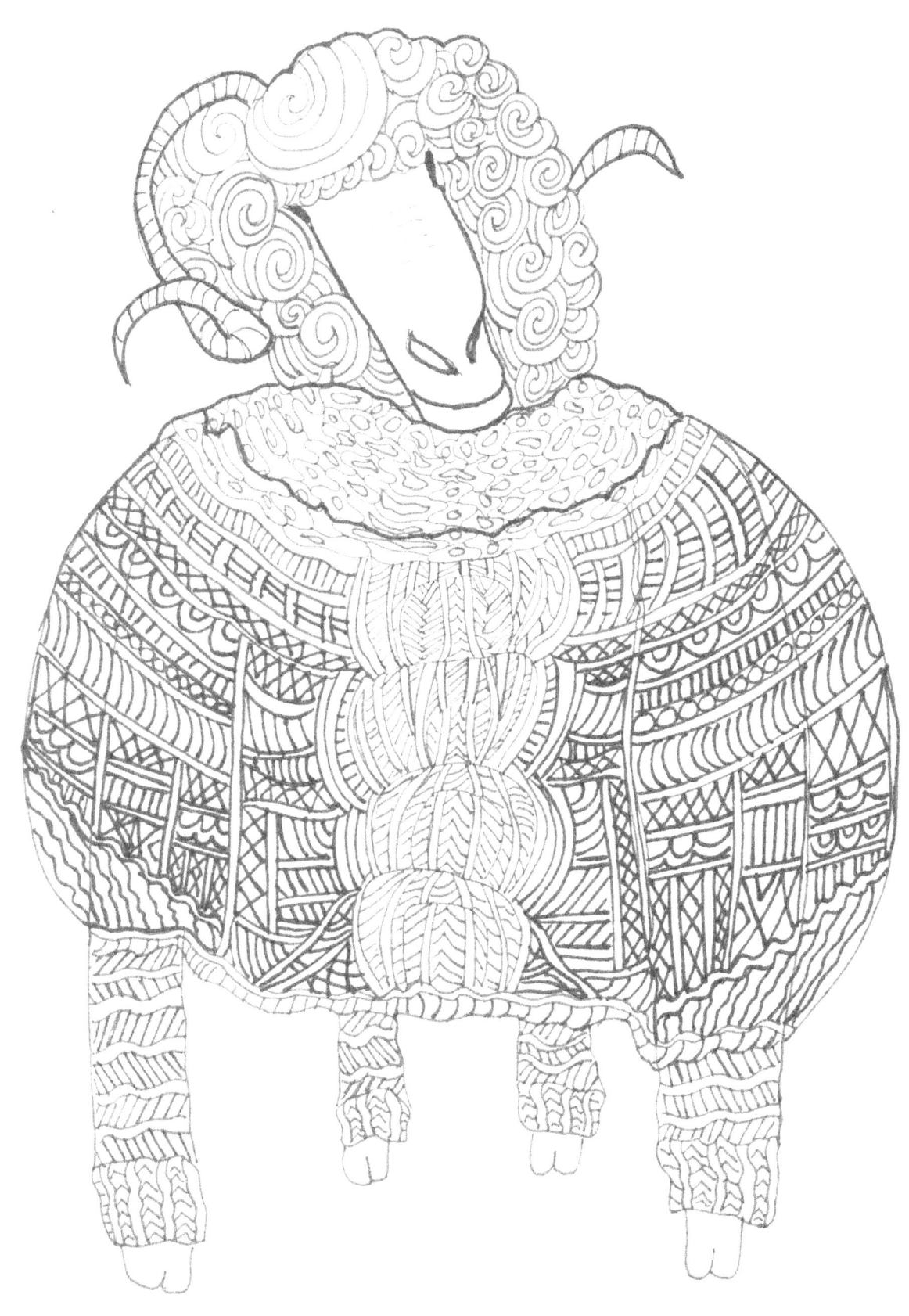

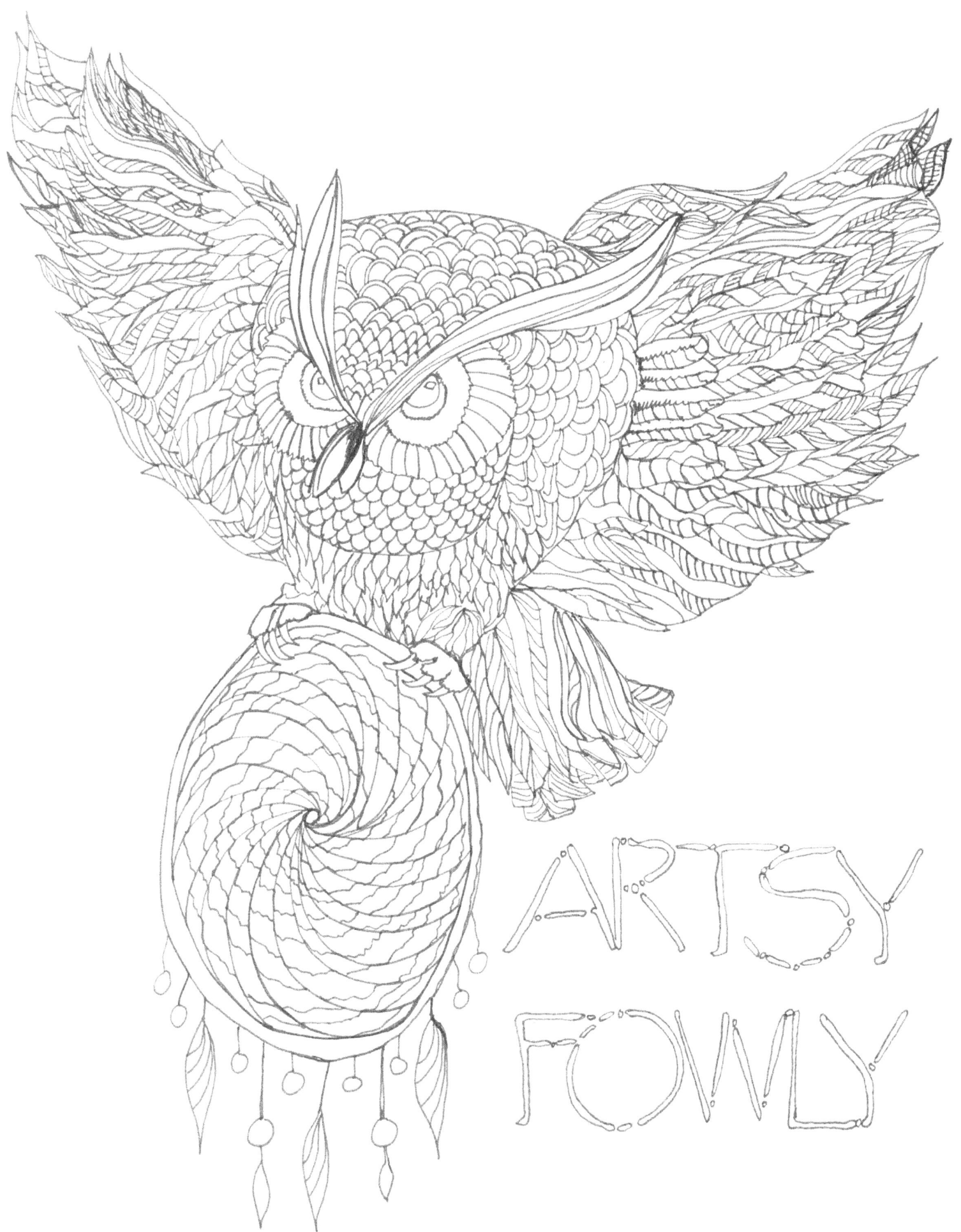

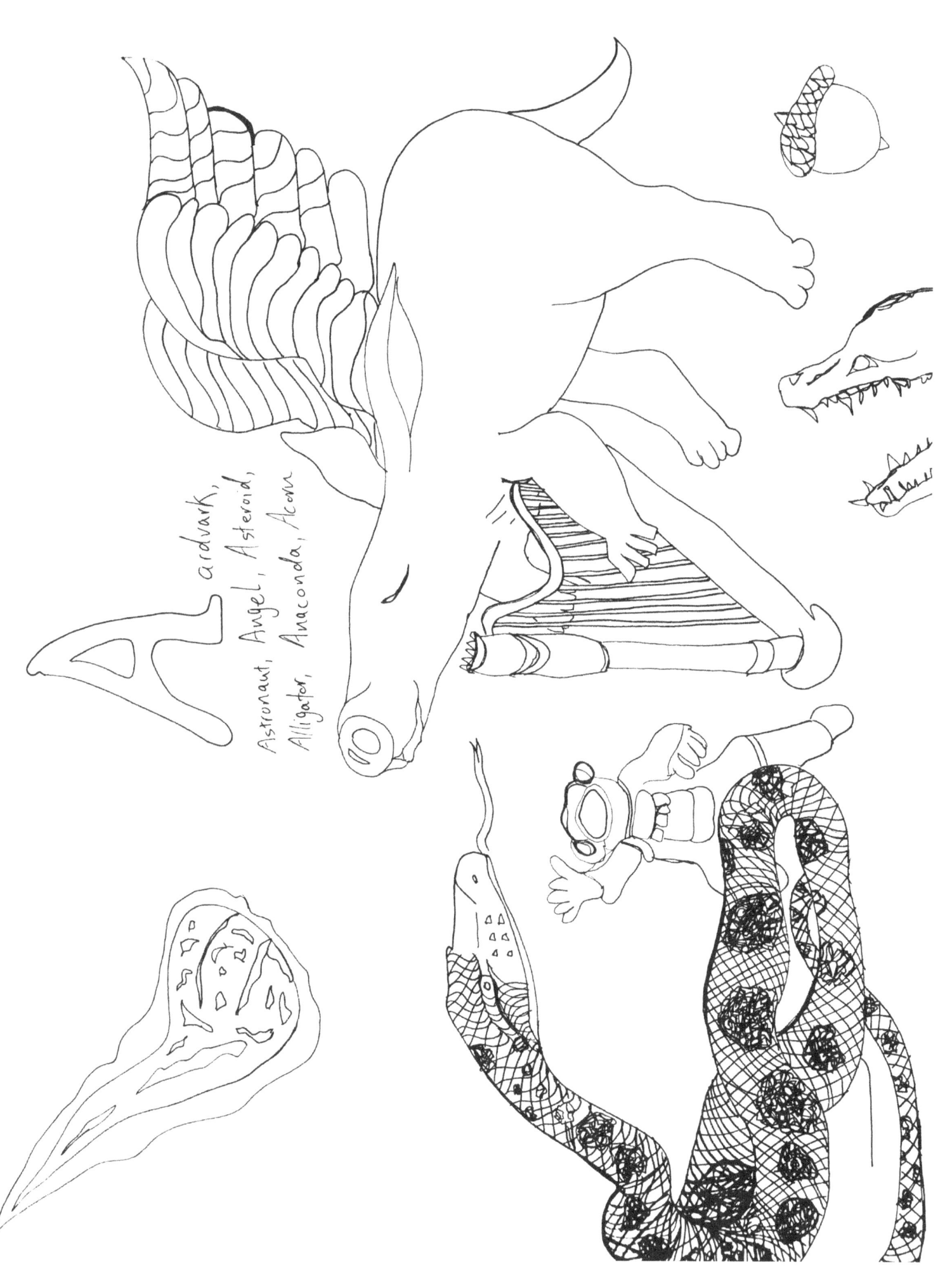

Aardvark,
Astronaut, Angel, Asteroid,
Alligator, Anaconda, Acorn

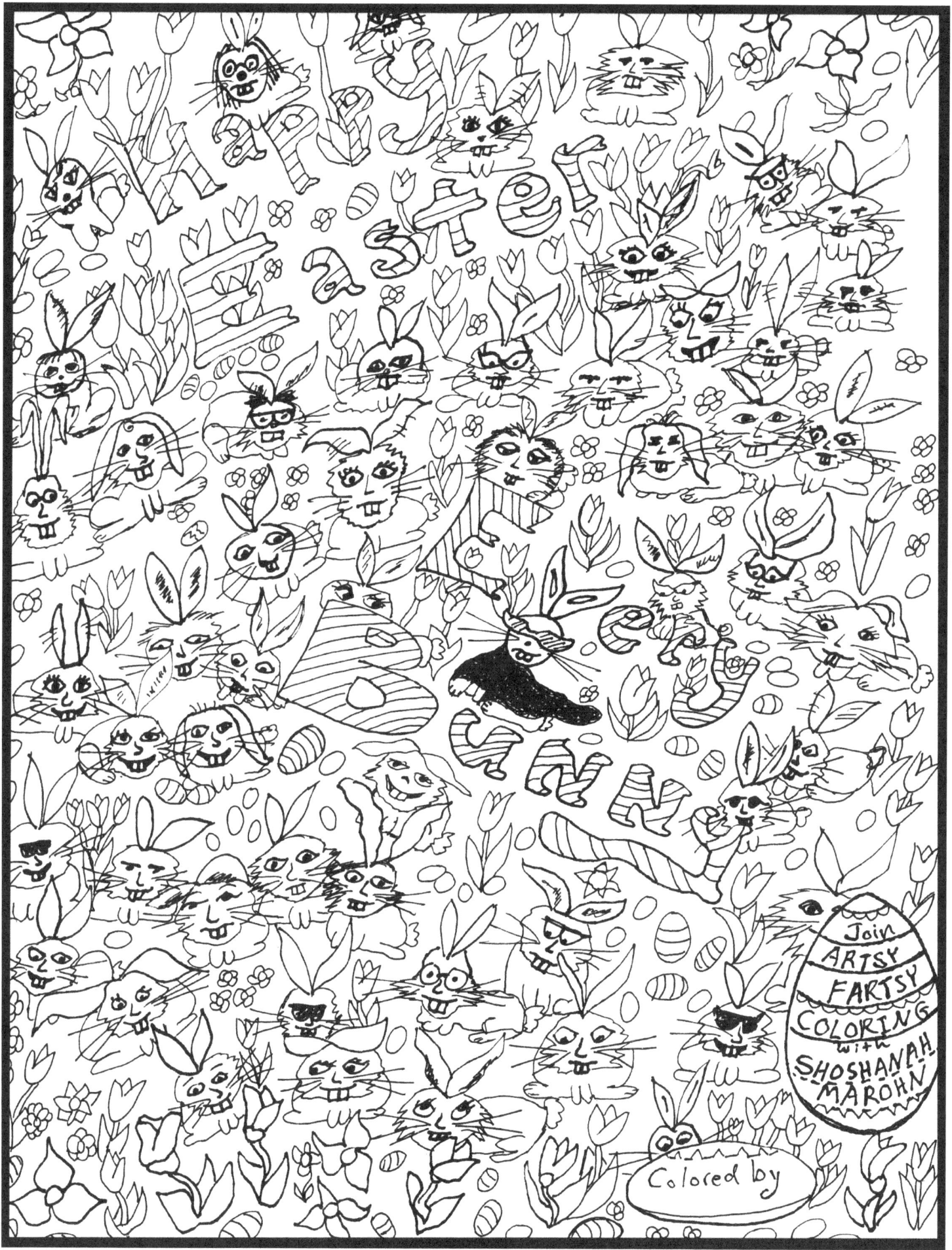

Join
ARTSY
FARTSY
COLORING
with
SHOSHANAH
MAROHN

Colored by

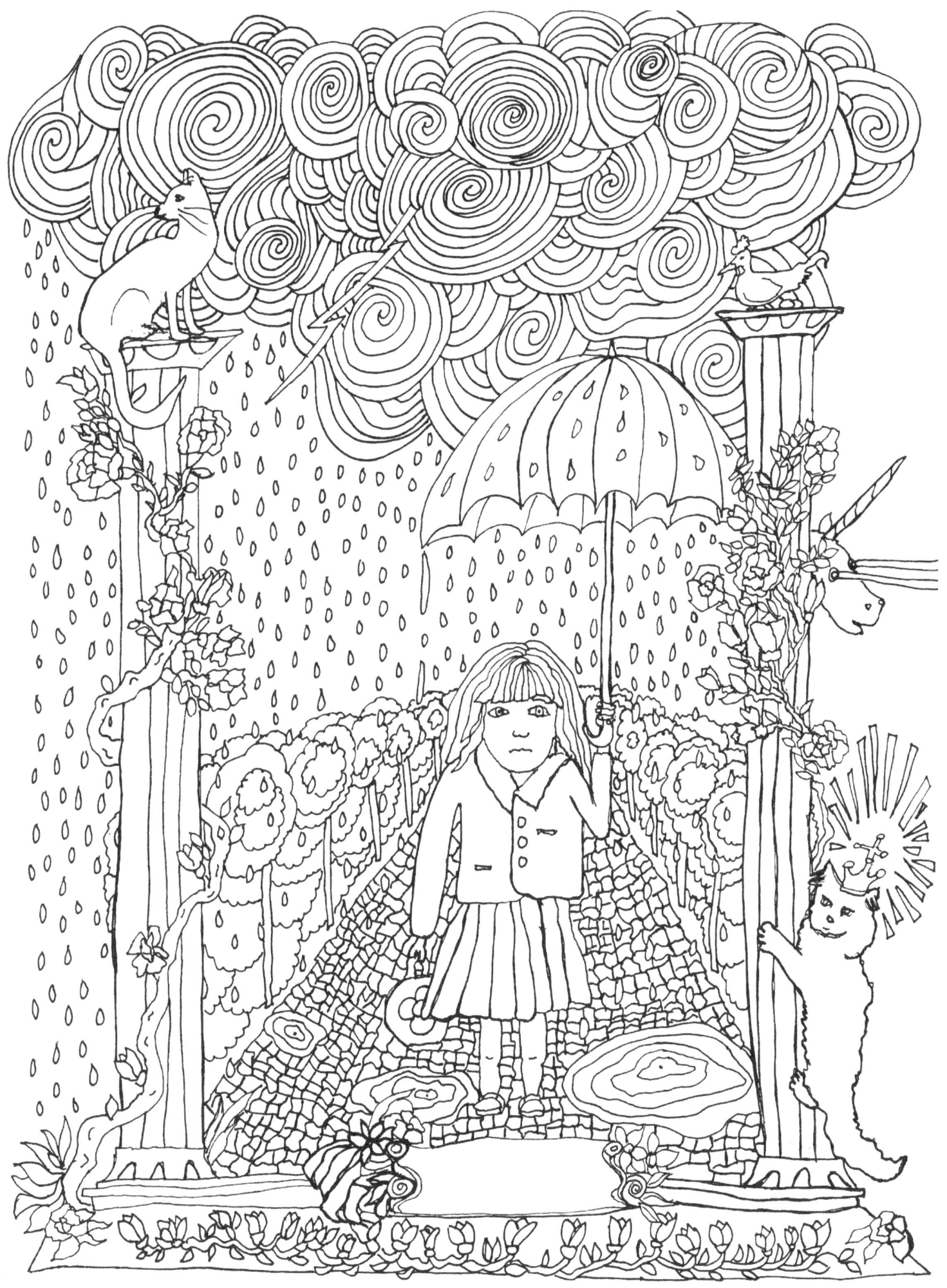

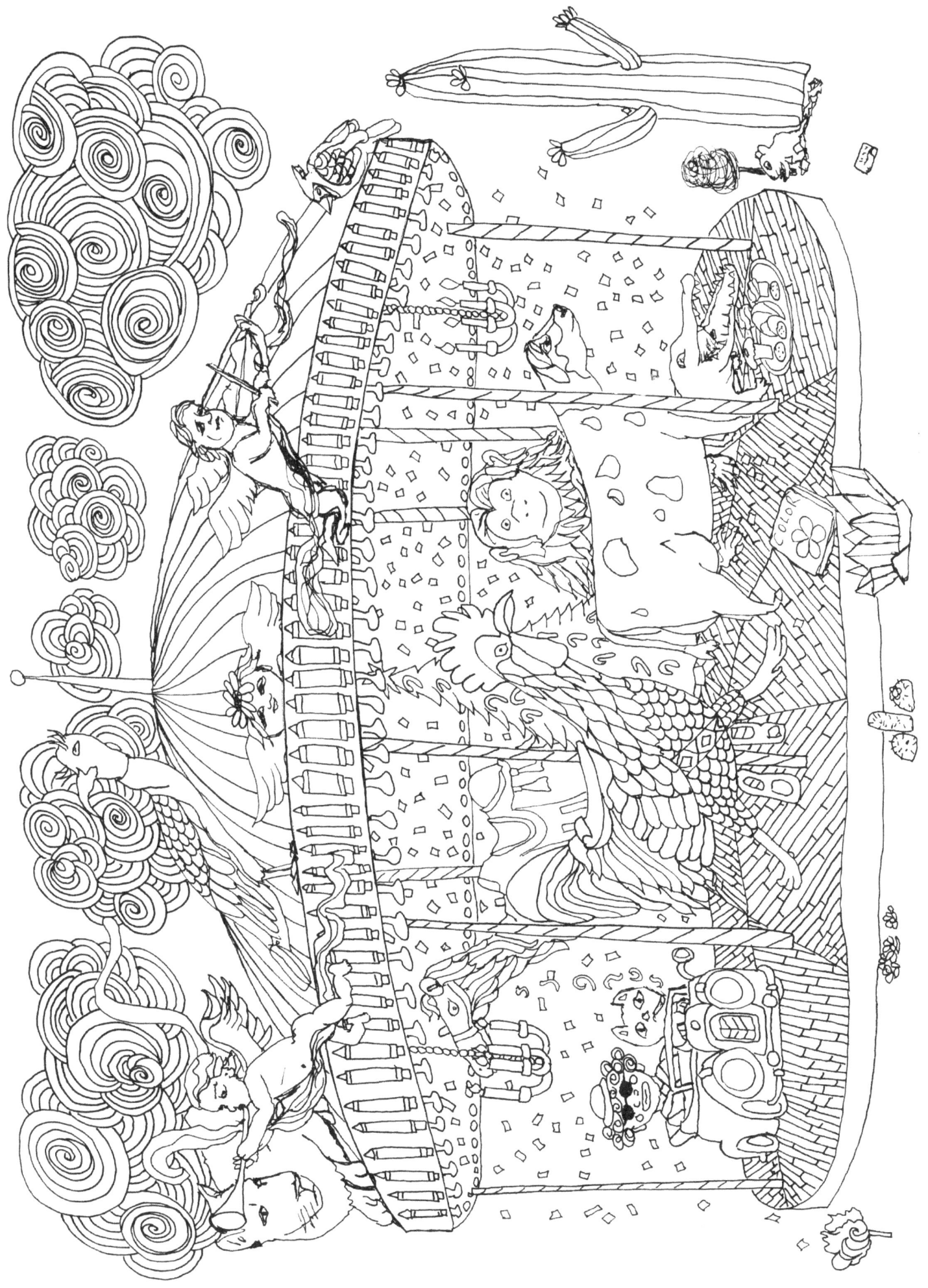

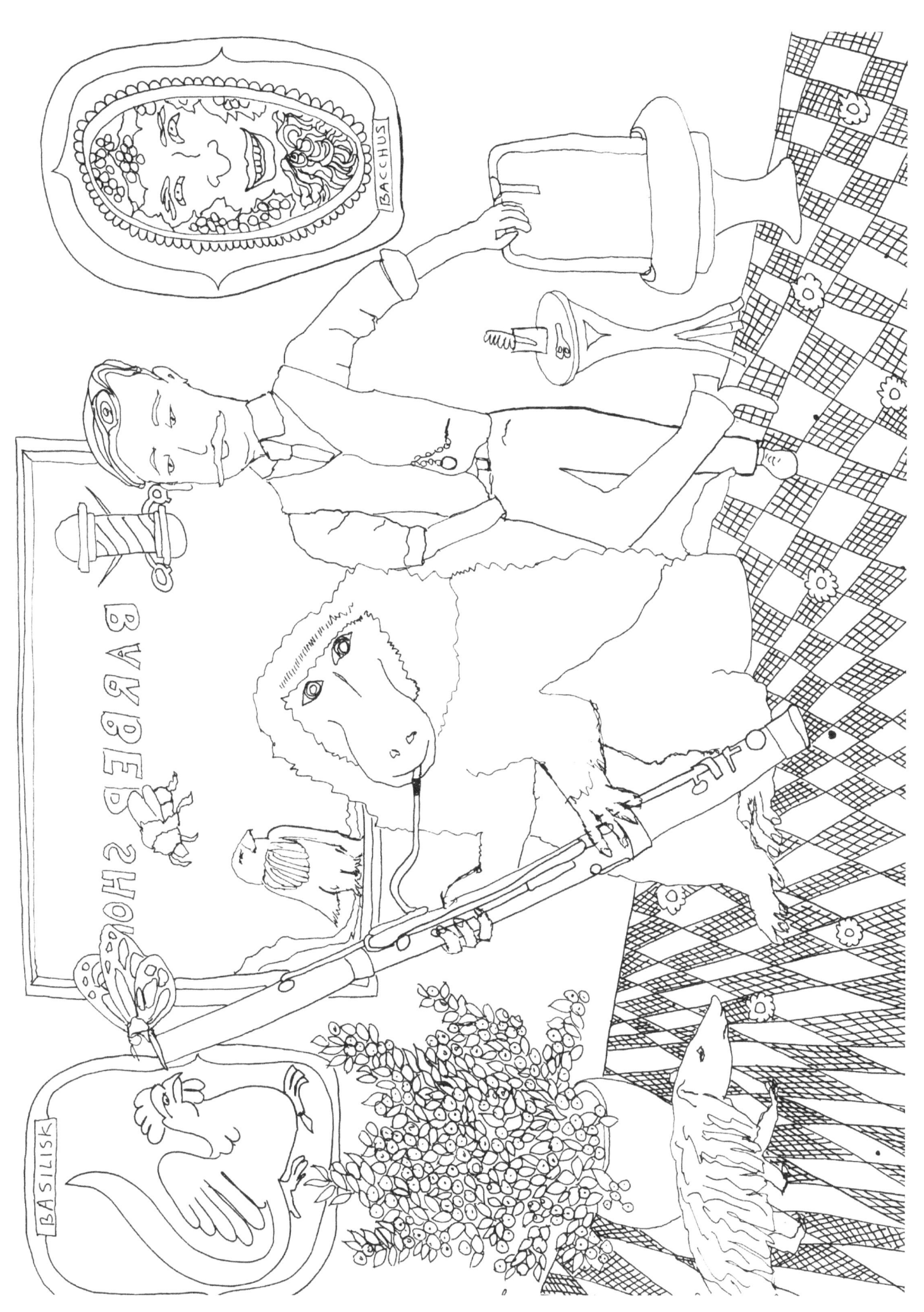

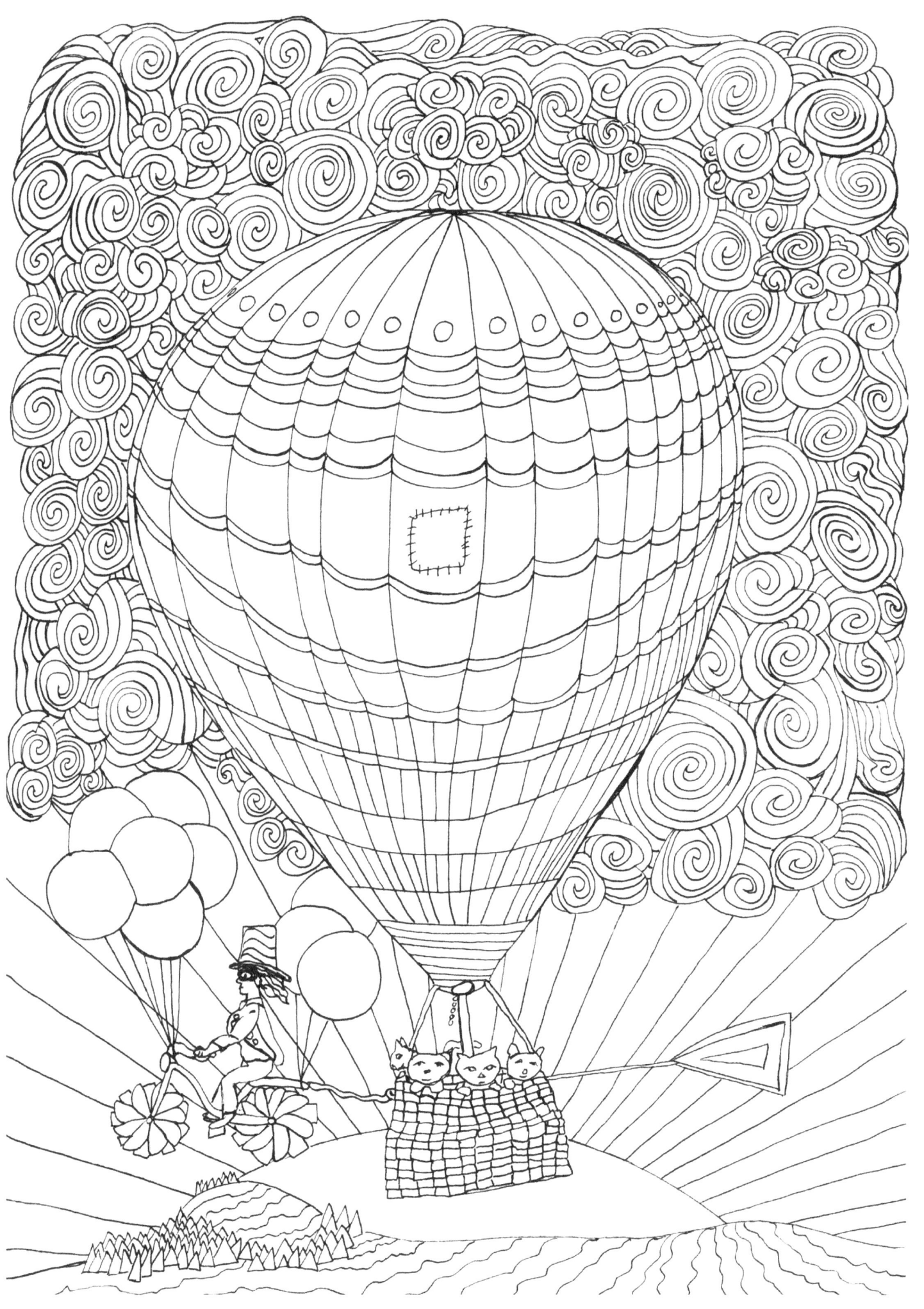

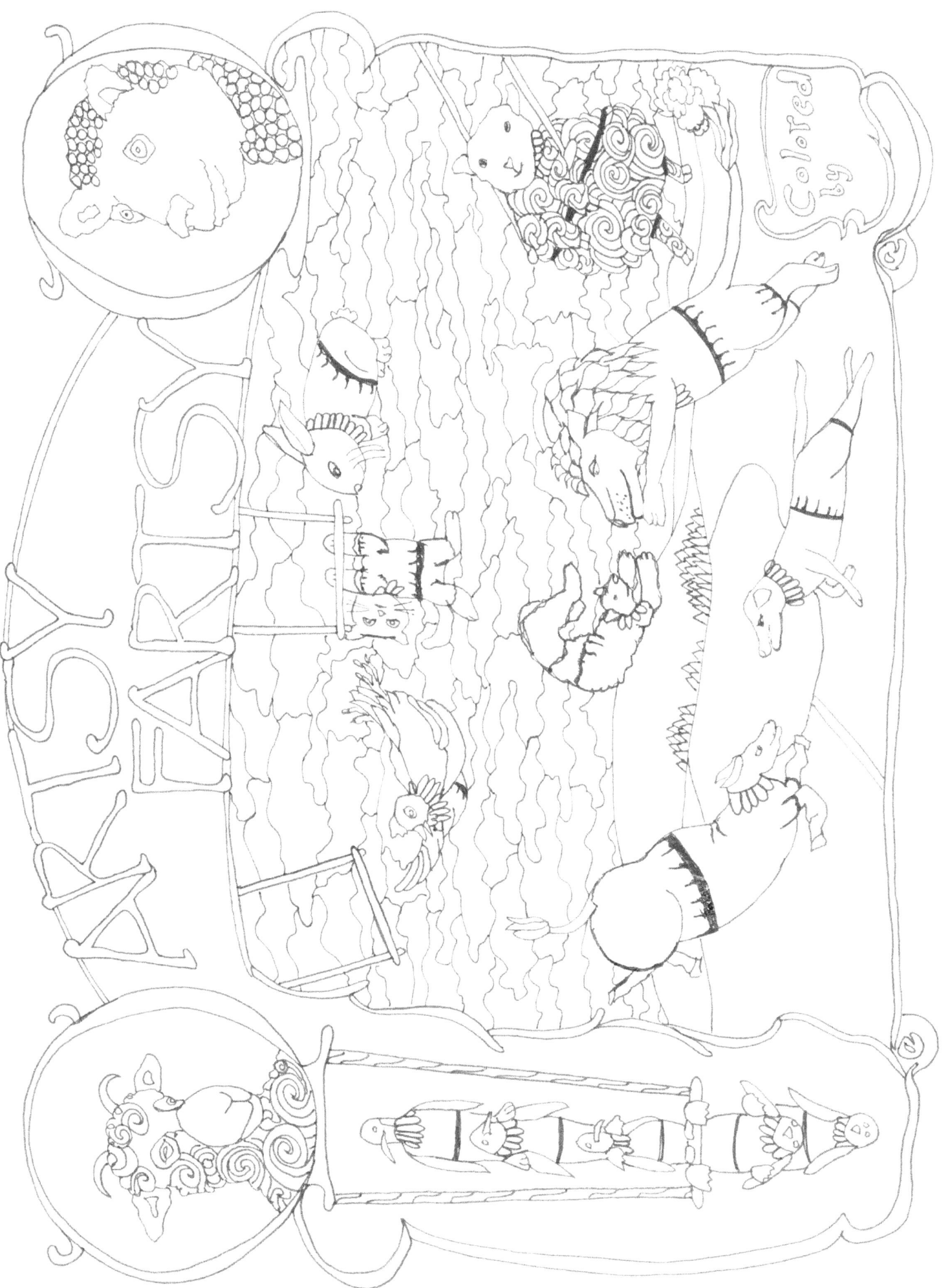

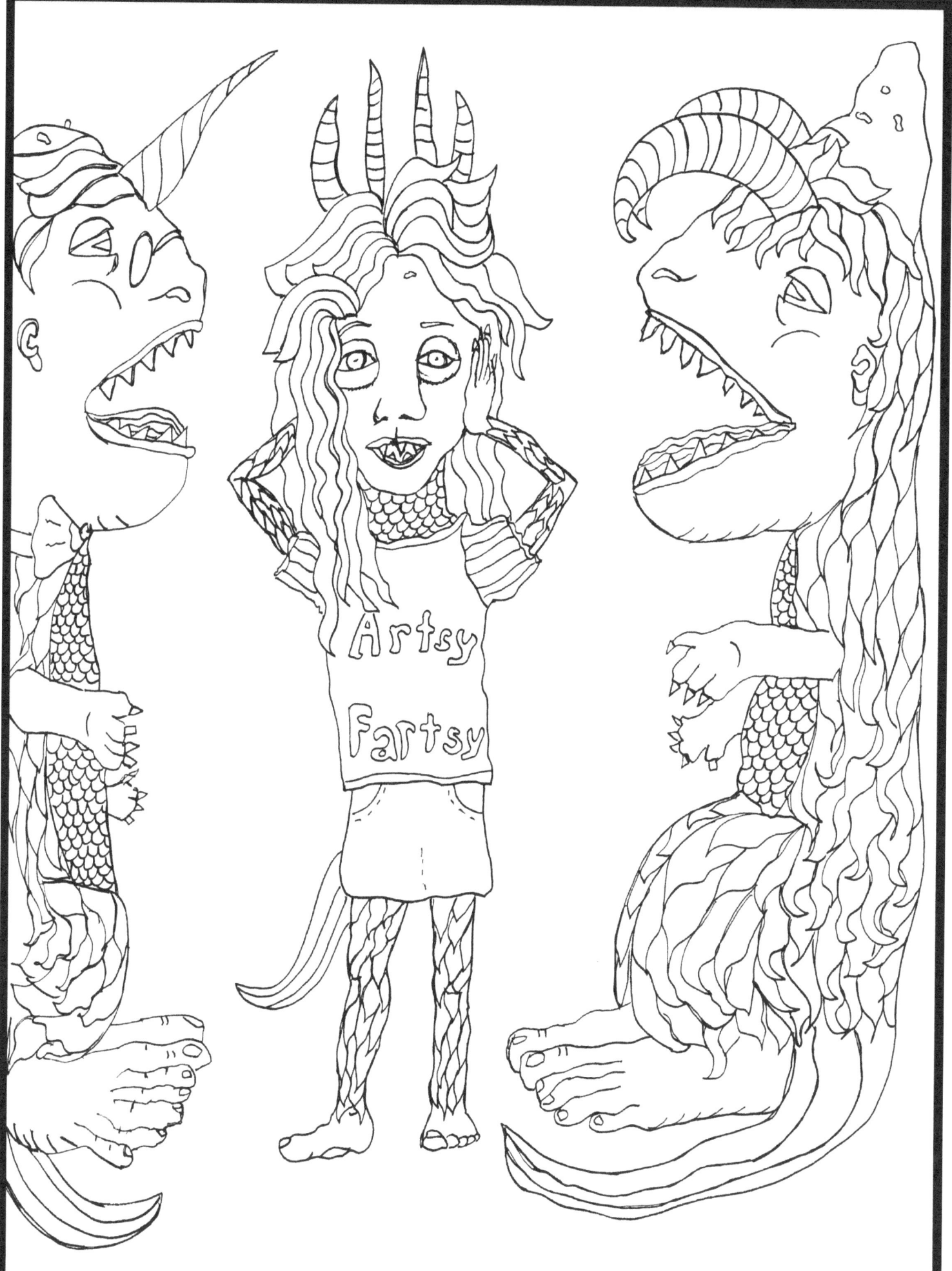

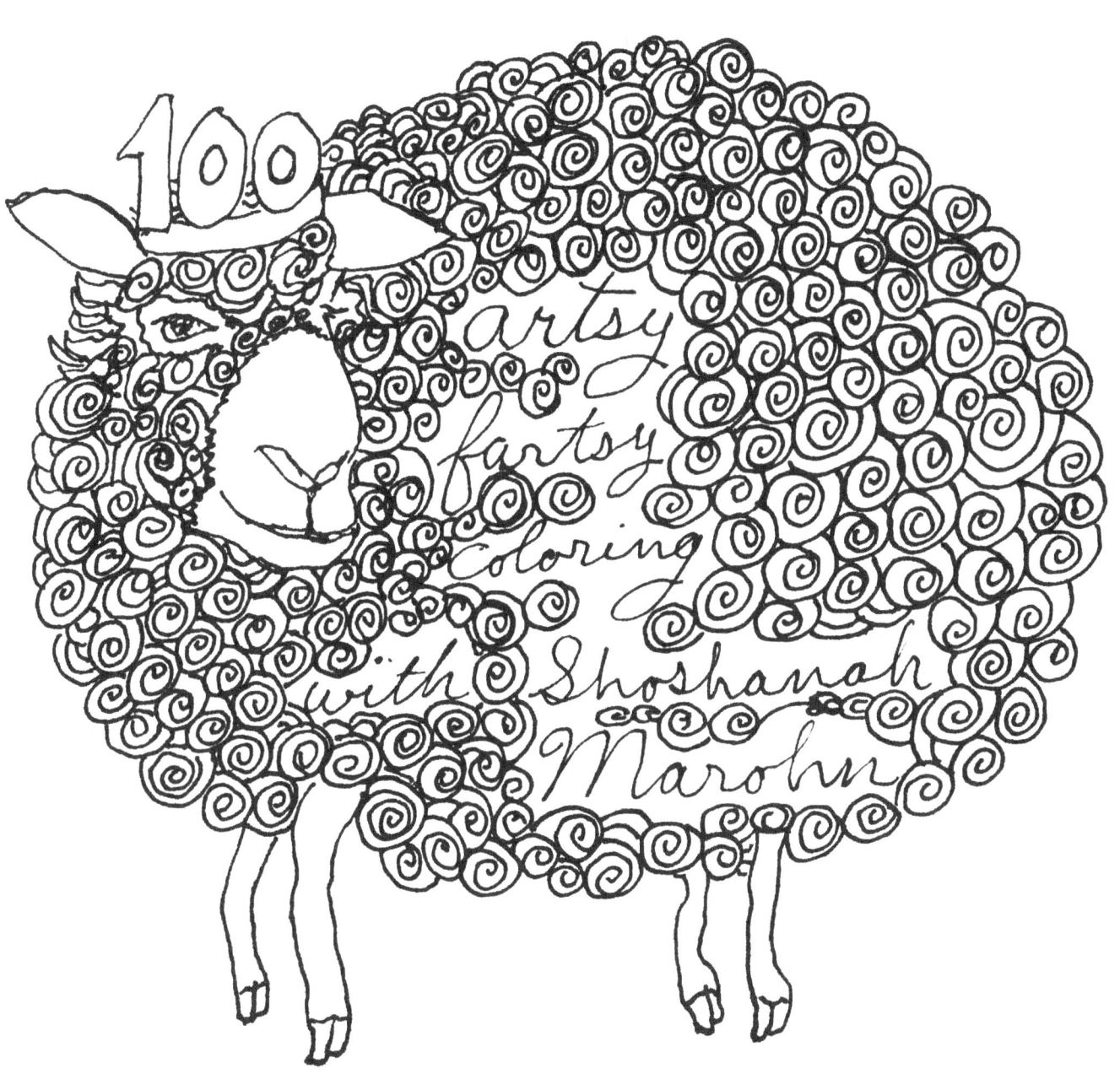

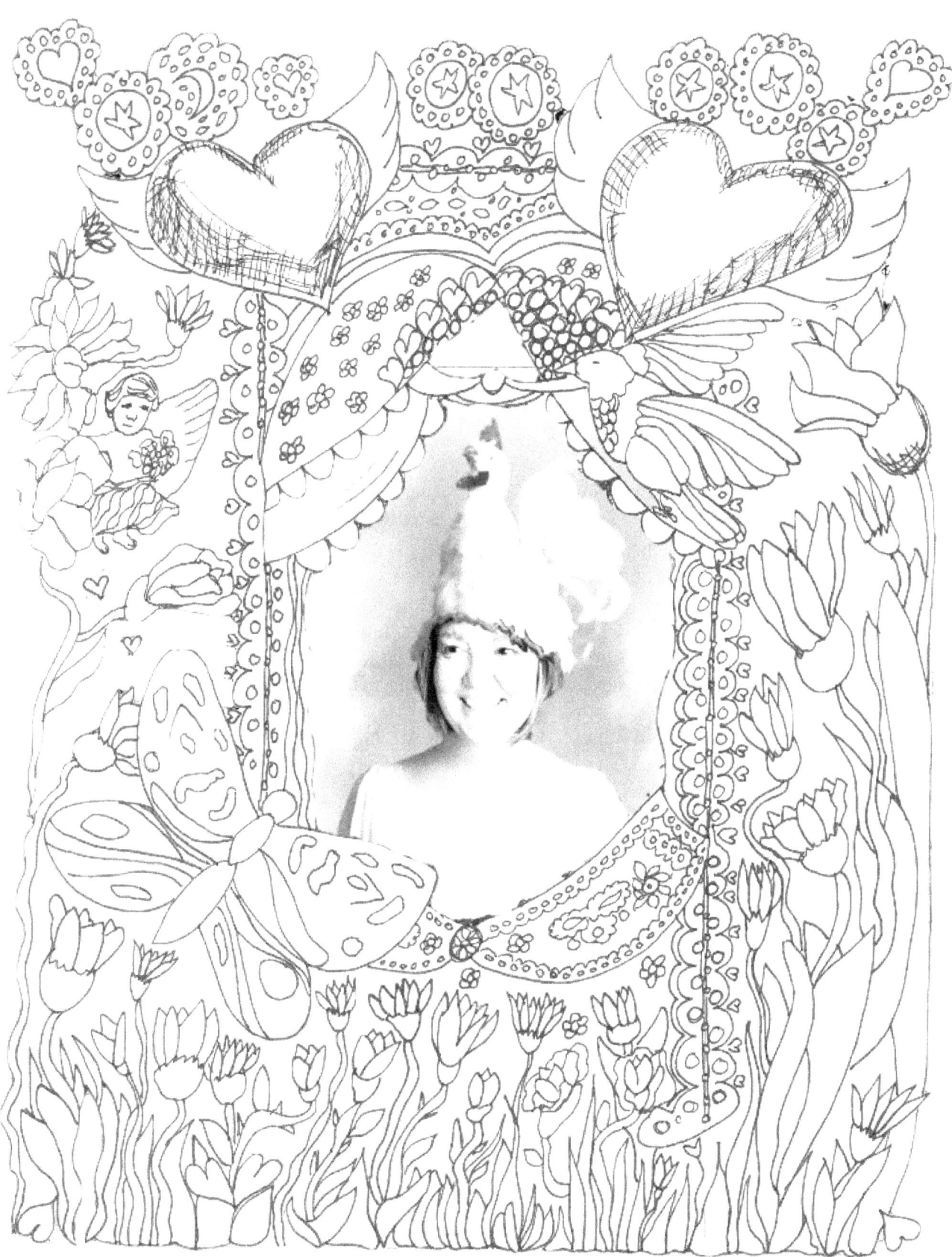

Illustrated by Shoshanah Marohn.

Join the coloring group at: https://www.facebook.com/groups/artsyfartsycoloringANDcolouring/

Other Books by Shoshanah Marohn

Coloring Books (In Order of Creation):

Coloring Inside the Dreams: http://geni.us/ColoringDreams

Birds in Beards Coloring Book: http://geni.us/Birds

The Tufa Coloring Book: http://geni.us/Tufa

Birds in Beards 2: Dead Poets Edition: http://geni.us/Birds2

The Trolls of Mount Horeb Coloring Book: http://geni.us/Trolls

Morbid Mandalas: A Creepy Coloring Book: http://geni.us/Morbid

Those Will KILL You!: Portraits of Colorists and Their Animals, Imagined and Real: http://geni.us/portraits

Children's Books:

A Murder of Crows and Other Woes: http://geni.us/murder

Murgatroyd Buttercups 1: http://geni.us/Murg

Murgatroyd Buttercups in Outer Space: http://geni.us/Unidog

Travel Novels:

Exhaust(ed): The 99% True Story of a Bus Trip Gone Wrong: http://geni.us/badbus

Avoiding Sex with Frenchmen: http://geni.us/ASWF

SHORTCUT TO MY ETSY PAGE:

https://tinyurl.com/artsyfartsyetsy

(The shop name is ShoshanahArt.)